A Purgatory of Misery

How Victorian Liberalism turned a crisis into a disaster

Frank Parker and Patrick Lillis

First published November 2017
Revised and reprinted December 2017

© Frank Parker, Patrick Lillis.

Also by Frank Parker

Honest Hearts
Summer Day
Strongbow's Wife
Transgression

except through a purgatory of misery and starvation, I cannot see how Ireland is to emerge into anything approaching either quiet or prosperity.

Charles Wood, Chancellor of the Exchequer in Lord John Russell's Whig government, approving the harsher measures contained in the Poor Law Extension Act of June 1847

Contents

Preface

Mary Marrinan was a teenager when she traveled from Miltown Malbay in County Clare to board the *Thomas Arbuthnot* in order to travel to Australia. She was one of over 4,000 such orphan girls, most aged between 14 and 19, who made the journey in eleven different vessels between October 1848 and August 1851. There was a shortage of women in the Colony. Ireland was wracked with famine. Such journeys were seen as a solution to both problems. The passengers paid nothing for their passage, instead the ship's operators were paid a bounty for each passenger.

In all it is estimated that a million men, women and children left Ireland during the famine years of 1845-51. Not all of them were as fortunate as Mary. Most will have travelled under conditions that, by today's standards, are unimaginable. Sharing the crossing from Ireland to Liverpool with a deck cargo of live cattle, or as ballast in the hold of a ship returning across the Atlantic after bringing grain or timber to Ireland.

As many died from starvation and/or disease in the same period. Reading the previous paragraph raises the question: why were Irish people starving when their livestock was being exported to England and grain being imported from North America?

Mary is one of Patrick Lillis's ancestors. She was one of the few who returned to Ireland. Many of the others married and produced large families in their new homes. Discovering her story is one of several incidents that inspired Patrick to learn more about the devastating famine that afflicted Ireland during those terrible years and to try to answer questions like the one posed at the end of the previous paragraph.

Among the other incidents that inspired Patrick was the singing of "The Fields of Athenry" by the crowd at an international football match in Poland during the 2014 European Cup Finals. The song is a lament by a young woman whose husband has been 'transported' as punishment for stealing corn. Another key moment came with the British Prime Minister Tony Blair's decision to express his regrets, on behalf of the British people, to the people of Ireland for his country's role in the tragedy.

We believe that it is impossible to gain an understanding of the events of 1845-51 without some knowledge of the relationship between Ireland and her neighbour that had evolved over the preceding 700 years or longer. That's why the first part of this book consists of a brief outline of those facts. We hope thereby to have provided some context for the otherwise inconceivable realities of mid-nineteenth century Ireland.

Those realities, covered in Part 2, are similarly viewed within the context of other events taking place simultaneously elsewhere in the United Kingdom and Europe.

Patrick met Frank Parker through the Laois writers group

and sought his assistance in researching and writing the book. We hope that we have produced something that will engender a deeper understanding of the Great Irish Famine such that lessons that have clearly not yet been learned are given greater weight in future decision making.

Acknowledgements

We cannot thank enough the members of the Laois Writers' Group for their encouragement under the leadership of Margaret Cotter. Ruth Coulson read an early draft of the manuscript and pointed out a number of minor errors. John Dorins provided valuable insights into the political sensitivity of certain geographical terms.

Authors' Note

The use of the term "British Isles" throughout this book is intended as a shorthand description of the group of islands that lies at the western edge of Europe. For reasons that will quickly become apparent to the reader, many Irish people have a deep resentment for any use of the word "British" in connection with their homeland. No offence is intended. This book is aimed at an international readership and we trust the term will be acceptable to the majority of such readers.

The same applies to the use of the expression "mainland" to distinguish the largest member of the group, including England, Scotland and Wales, from the island of Ireland.

Introduction

Potato Blight *(phytophthora infestans)* first appeared on the eastern seaboard of the United States of America in 1843, spreading north, west and south from New York. The following year its outward spread had reached Montreal and the south eastern tip of Lake Ontario. By 1845 it had reached Chicago, Washington and the whole of New Foundland.

It reached Europe in June the same year, spreading east from the Belgian coast as far as Frankfurt in Germany. By August that year it had reached the south coast of England. Its spread in that unusually damp summer was rapid. By the end of September it was evident across an area stretching south to the Pyranees, north to Scandinavia and affecting the whole of the British Isles.

That year, it was the eastern part of Ireland that was most affected, some areas escaping the full impact of the disease. In 1846 almost the whole crop was destroyed.

Given that the disease affected such a wide area, why is it that Ireland suffered far more than any other part of Europe or North America?

The answer, we believe, is to be found in a study of the peculiar geography of the island, its history and social organisation and, most significantly, the relationship between the peoples of Ireland and the governing class of its neighbour.

The story really begins in that period of history often referred to as 'The Dark Ages', broadly speaking, the period between the collapse of the Roman Empire and the arrival on British soil of William, Duke of Normandy, in 1066. It was a period that saw successive attempts to invade the British Isles from mainland Europe and Scandinavia. It was the latter which was most successful. The Vikings established settlements along the east coasts of England and of Ireland, and the N

north coast of modern France.

It was their occupation of eastern England that precipitated the union of three provinces – Wessex, Mercia and Northumbria – under a single leader, the legendary King Alfred.

In Ireland the Norse, as they were known, occupied Dublin, Wexford and Waterford. The King of Leinster was acknowledged as the man with responsibility for ensuring their confinement to those cities, where they established themselves as merchants overseeing a thriving trade between the island, mainland Britain and further afield.

Those who had settled in northern France, where their territory became known as Normandy, never gave up their attempts to expand north into England. It was this ambition that culminated in what the English would ever afterwards refer to as 'the Norman conquest', or simply 'the Conquest'.

In Ireland, outside the Norse settlements, the various clans of Celts were constantly at war with each other. They were for the most part a semi-nomadic people, herding cattle and growing grain, mainly oats and barley. Each group had its King. These Kings fought for the right to be 'High King', the most senior leader.

They were governed by a sophisticated set of laws, known as Brehon Law. Another source of conflict was the divergence of these traditional laws from the laws of the Church. Kings, in Ireland and the mainland alike, sought to keep favour with the Church by endowing Abbeys. This gave them a voice in the selection of Church leaders.

These Irish clans also made occasional forays across the sea to the South-West of England. On one such raid, not long after the departure of the Romans from British soil, they captured the son of a Romano-British aristocrat and Churchman. He was sold into slavery and spent six years in the Irish province of Ulster as a herdsman, before escaping and going to France where, in due course, he was ordained and became a missionary, returning to bring Christianity to the Irish. He established a monastery on the Island of Iona off the west coast of Scotland. His name reflects his belief that he was of the aristocracy. *Patricius* – the patrician – became the founding father of the Church in Ireland.

The Normans in England, post 1066, had little inclination to expand beyond the coast of Wales. Indeed, they had enough trouble keeping the Welsh and Scots in check. A number of Norman families had been granted lands in England. Some of those closest to William were given land along the border between England and Wales on condition that they provided the man-power necessary to resist raiding parties led by Welsh Princes.

A hundred years after the conquest all that changed. The Pope had issued a request to the King of England, Henry II, asking him to provide military support in his dispute with the Church in Ireland that was, he believed, making too many concessions to the Brehon traditions. The King was reluctant to become involved. He was embroiled in his own dispute with the Church over the question of whose laws – the Church's or the King's – took precedence. His hand was forced by a dispute over the High Kingship of Ireland.

The King of Leinster, Dermot McMurrough, had laid claim to the supreme crown but had been defeated in battle by a neighbouring coalition that had succeeded in deposing him from his title as King of Leinster. He decided to use his contacts with a merchant in Bristol that he knew had the ear of King Henry. That merchant introduced him to Richard DeClare, nicknamed Strongbow. It took a while, but in 1171/2 Henry II annexed Ireland and allocated large tracts of land to Norman families, many of them the same people who had been protecting the border with Wales.

Ireland was, from then on, a part of what would

become over succeeding centuries, the greatest empire the world has ever known.

Part 1 – Context

Chapter 1 – History

It took three years – and the offer of his daughter's hand in marriage – for Dermot McMurrough to persuade Strongbow to come to Ireland. Once there, his success was a source of worry for Henry II. Henry ordered him to return and ordered ships' captains to remain in port, preventing supplies from reaching the Island. When that failed he determined to come to Ireland in person. With him were 400 ships carrying *Enormous quantities of wheat and oats ... with a supply of hand-mills for milling flour while on the move. Beans, salt, cheese and a vast amount of bacon ... Cloth in large quantities was supplied for the troops ... coarse grey woollen cloth suitable for the dampness of an Irish winter. But the king was expected to dress in better finery ... 25 ells of scarlet cloth, 26 ells of green, 12 pieces of silk cloth, 2 skins of mountain cats and 5 otter skins.* There was also an *enormous quantity of timber and nails* as well as *axes spades and pickaxes ... in great numbers.*[1]

He arrived in Waterford on the 17th or 18th of October 1171. With him came around 500 knights and 4,000 others, mostly archers. As things turned out not an arrow was fired. The size of the force was sufficient to intimidate the majority of Irish kings who submitted to Henry, as he progressed around the country, without a fight. Perhaps they trusted him to restrain

Strongbow and leave them to look after their own affairs in his name. More probably they did what they had always done in their disputes with each other – made promises they had no intention of keeping.

Certainly, Strongbow's wings were clipped. When Henry returned to England at Easter 1172, he appointed Hugh DeLacy to the governorship of Ireland. Garrisons were established under the command of various of the knights who had accompanied the king. These men took land from its native Irish owners, in the name of the king. However, in 1173, Strongbow, DeLacy and the rest were called to Normandy to help Henry put down a rebellion led by his wife and sons. Not surprisingly, the Irish took advantage of the situation and re-occupied the stolen lands.

Henry reacted by appointing Strongbow as his commander in Ireland, with Raymond FitzGerald (aka Le Gros) as his lieutenant. Fitzgerald was the man who had master-minded the massacre of the citizens of Waterford days before Strongbow's first arrival and marriage to McMurough's daughter. The stage was set for the kind of retribution that would be repeated time and again over succeeding centuries.

Neither the Irish, nor the descendants of the original Norman occupation force, were ever allowed to get on with running their own affairs. Violent disputes continued on mainland Britain and these frequently spilled over into Ireland. In the 14th century, for example, the brother of a Scottish king, himself a descendant of one of the Norman nobles who accompanied Duke William's invasion of England, conducted a devastating campaign in Ireland in the midst of a famine.

Several accounts of this Scottish invasion and famine refer to people turning to cannibalism in a desperate attempt to overcome their hunger. The Annals of Conaught, for example, say of this period that *for three years and a half, falsehood and famine and homicide filled the country, and undoubtedly men ate each other in Ireland.*[2]

As was to happen in the nineteenth century, grains were imported from Ireland to England. On this occasion it was to supply troops fighting the Scots. There were other forms of assistance provided from the Anglo-Norman colony to their cousins in England. Historians have suggested that the most likely reason for Edward Bruce's Irish expedition was to prevent this trade. It is also the case that his invasion was supported by a significant contingent of native Irish. Together the Scots and Irish hoped to defeat the Anglo-Normans once and for all.

Whatever his motives, the campaign proved to be a disaster for Bruce's army and his Irish Allies. The decisive battle took place near Athenry in August 1316. A force of some 8,000 Irish, led by Felim O'Connor, were defeated by a smaller force led by William 'Liath' DeBurg. It was to prove to be the final victory for the Anglo-Normans. Up to that point they had controlled only the part of Ireland east of the Shannon, whilst the Irish maintained power in the west. Now the Connaught Irish were fatally weakened.

The famine that coincided with Bruce's campaign was caused by a sequence of very wet summers which destroyed crops, not only in Ireland but across the British Isles and much of Europe. It prevented the English from invading Scotland on this occasion, suggesting that Bruce need not have bothered. Instead the famine devastated his army. One account, from a Dublin chronicler, suggests that the Anglo-Irish occupiers of a garrison at Carrickfergus killed and ate some of their Scottish prisoners.

If the second battle of Athenry, as it came to be known because there had been an earlier, though less bloody, battle in the same vicinity, resulted in defeat for the Irish, it was certainly not a victory for the English. Already many of the Anglo-Normans in Ireland were beginning to think of themselves as Irish. The Butlers, Fitzgeralds and Burkes raised their own armed forces, enforced their own law, and adopted Gaelic language and culture. By the middle of the 16th Century many of them were as much opposed to rule from London as were the native Irish, many of whom had re-taken large areas of land previously held by authority of the English crown, particularly in the north and midlands.

English rule was reduced to an area covered by a radius of some 50 kilometres from Dublin, called 'The Pale'. The Fitzgeralds led several rebellions against English rule, one of which ended with yet another famine, this time instigated as a deliberate policy by the English who destroyed crops. The poet, Edmund Spenser, who served in the English army at the bloody siege of Smerwick and received lands in County Cork for his trouble, later wrote a pamphlet advocating the widespread adoption of such a policy. He included a description of what he had seen in the aftermath of the campaign:

"Out of everye corner of the woode and glenns they came creepinge forth upon theire handes, for theire legges could not beare them; they looked Anatomies [of] death, they spake like ghostes, crying out of theire graves; they did eate of the carrions, happye wheare they could find them, yea, and one another soone after, in soe much as the verye carcasses they spared not to scrape out of theire graves; and if they found a plott of water-cresses or shamrockes, theyr they flocked as to a feast… in a shorte space there were none almost left, and a most populous and plentyfull countrye suddenly lefte voyde of man or beast: yett sure in all that warr, there perished not manye by the sworde, but all by the extreamytie of famine … they themselves had wrought"[3]

The solution adopted, first by Queen Mary and then by her half-sister Queen Elizabeth, was 'Plantation', the confiscation of lands and their reallocation to supposedly loyal English and Scottish families.

Spenser's pamphlet was not published until some years after his death. It describes a proposed system of governance based on that already in force in England but with one crucial difference: the posting of troops in every administrative centre. It may well be that he was describing what he had seen, for that is more or less what happened.

By the middle of the seventeenth century the English were as disenchanted with the monarchy as were the Irish. Unfortunately the regime that came to power briefly, following the execution of King Charles I, was of no benefit to Ireland. Indeed, Oliver Cromwell instigated a campaign of terror across the island. Many Irish landowners had joined with Royalists in a plan to invade England and restore Charles to the throne. In response, a Parliamentarian army landed in Ireland. The ensuing war produced many atrocities on both sides but it was the civilian population that suffered most.

Once again a policy of destruction of crops was carried out, leading to famine. An outbreak of bubonic plague added to the misery of the people. Estimates of the loss of life during the period 1649-53 vary. There is no doubt that upwards of 300,000 died out of a pre-war population of 1.4 million. At least 50,000 prisoners of war were sent to semi-slavery in the British colonies in North America and the Caribbean. Land was confiscated and re-settled by English Parliamentarian war veterans and the English merchants who had financed the campaign. Many Irish fighting men left to join the French or Spanish armies.

After the restoration of the English monarchy in 1660, about a third of the confiscated lands were returned to their original owners. The relationship between king and parliament had undergone a fundamental change as a result of the Civil War and Charles II needed to keep his old enemies on side. When he died, trouble brewed once again in England over who should succeed him. And once again Ireland became embroiled, causing great suffering to the ordinary people and deepening the rift between long established residents and new arrivals.

[*This is a deliberately brief summary of the Cromwellian campaign, its background and aftermath. Because of the strongly religious elements that underpinned it, a more detailed account will be provided in chapter 2.*]

There is one final episode that sets the scene for the events of 1845-51. Throughout the eighteenth century England was involved in wars with France and Spain. It was also a period of revolutions, in France and in America, in particular. Many in Ireland were inspired to seek the establishment of an independent republic and to do so with the assistance of England's enemy, France. A group called The United Irishmen, formed in 1791 and driven underground three years later when the government discovered they were negotiating with the French, continued to plot and plan. In December 1796 a French fleet carrying 14,000 troops arrived off the south coast of Ireland. Rough seas prevented its landing.

The government responded by infiltrating the organisation with spies and informants and strengthening its defences against a possible further French invasion. The United Irishmen showed their hand by seizing mail coaches leaving Dublin on the night of 25/26 May 1798. Rebel groups around the country went into action but were easily defeated by superior government forces, except in Wexford. The final battle took place at Vinegar Hill, outside Enniscorthy, on June 21st. As so often in the past, there were many atrocities committed on both sides but the rebellion was firmly put down. An 1100 strong French force landed in County Mayo in August and took Castlebar but surrendered shortly afterward. The French were treated as prisoners of war but those Irish who had supported them were massacred. Between 10,000 and 25,000 rebels lost their lives in the 1798 rebellion. The government in London, believing that failings in its Dublin outpost had contributed to the rebellion, decided that Ireland should become an integral part of a new United Kingdom of Great Britain and Ireland, governed directly from London.

Chapter 2 – Religion

The previous chapter provided a summary of how the political relationship between Ireland and its neighbour developed over the seven centuries preceding the famine. But that is only a part of the story. We have already indicated that religious thought and argument, especially in regard to the question of the power of kings versus that of the Pope, was central to the lives of secular and spiritual leaders.

Years before Dermot McMurrough, the deposed king of Leinster, set out to seek English assistance, the Pope had signalled his dissatisfaction with the behaviour of some of his bishops in Ireland. Indeed, the fact that Dermot paid a visit to the Papal Legate in Lismore before setting sail suggests that he had that fact in mind and intended to use it as leverage in his plea to King Henry. The murder of Arch-Bishop Becket by knights loyal to him meant that the king felt the need to atone. And what better way than by carrying out an instruction that he had so far ignored?

But the native Irish continued to cling to their ancient traditions and the Brehon laws. And quite a few of the conquering Anglo-Normans adopted them too. Until the sixteenth century it was battles over the English royal succession and war with France that preoccupied the authorities in England, occasionally spilling over into Ireland, as in the Bruce invasion in the 14th century. But in the 1500s Europe was gripped by a movement for reform of the Church. Led by men like Martin Luther, this movement was opposed to the power wielded by the clergy, seeking greater democracy for the Church, with bibles and liturgy in native languages and an end to reverence for religious relics and symbols.

As part of this movement the old argument about the right of kings to have sovereignty over the clergy once again came to the fore. England's king, another Henry, the eighth to carry the name, took advantage of the movement in order to secure a divorce from his first wife who had failed to provide him with the son he desired as heir. The practices of the Church of England which he declared as independent from Rome were, to begin with, little changed from those of the Roman Catholic church.

Church lands and property were now crown assets and were re-distributed among the English aristocracy, in Ireland as well as in England. Tithes continued to be paid but to the newly established Church of England and, in Ireland, Church of Ireland.

Meanwhile, the so-called Protestant movement continued to grow. Following Henry's death the son his third wife, Jane Seymore, had produced, came to power. Like his mother, Edward was an ardent supporter of the movement and set about the destruction of monasteries and the wholesale murder of those who opposed him. His reign was mercifully short. He was succeeded by his half-sister Mary who had remained true to her mother's Roman Catholicism. As it turned out, this fact was no help to Ireland. As already noted in Chapter 1, it was Mary who was the first to introduce the practice of confiscating Irish land and 'planting' English loyalists.

Following Mary's death it was the turn of the other half-sister, Elizabeth, to rule over England. Elizabeth's reign is usually seen in England as one of progress and prosperity characterised by exploration and discovery. And the successful overthrowing of the Spanish Armada, much of which came to grief on the north-west coast of Ireland. But it was not a good time to be a Roman Catholic anywhere in the archipelago, and priests, if discovered, risked imprisonment or worse.

Throughout Ireland Mass was celebrated in secret places in the open air, in woodlands or on mountain sides where a rocky outcrop would be dedicated as a makeshift altar to be referred to, to this day as a Mass Rock. And in many English country houses there are small, dark spaces called 'priest holes'. These were the places where priests hid whenever priest hunters were in the neighbourhood.

Nicholas Owen was the most skilled and prolific builder of priest holes. A Jesuit brother, Owen dedicated his life to constructing secret chambers to protect the lives of Catholic priests. In the book, Alan Fea describes how he artfully designed and created priest hides:

"With incomparable skill, he knew how to conduct priests to a place of safety along subterranean passages, to hide them

between walls and bury them in impenetrable recesses, and to entangle them in labyrinths and a thousand windings".[1]

In Ireland the practice of 'planting' of Protestant farmers in Ireland was stepped up, especially in Ulster.

The dissatisfaction with the monarchy in the middle of the seventeenth century referred to in Chapter 1 was principally based on a distrust of Charles I and his alliances with, and support for, those who seemed to many to be taking the Church of England back to the old, Catholic, ways. Parliament wanted to see the Church adopt the practices and beliefs of Presbyterianism. The Scots were, by now, mostly of the same persuasion, so when the king sought funding to resist a Scottish invasion, Parliament refused. Instead they agreed to Scottish demands that certain named individuals be charged with treason.

In Ireland there were now three distinct factions: Native Irish, 'Old English' (descendants of the original Norman settlers and mostly Catholic) and 'New English', the occupiers of confiscated lands. The king's representative in Ireland, Thomas Wentworth, had operated a harsh regime and continued with confiscations and plantations. Nevertheless, he had succeeded in maintaining an uneasy peace between the factions. When Parliament refused the king's request for support for a campaign against the Scots, Wentworth suggested raising an Irish force to invade Scotland on the king's behalf. Not surprisingly it was

Wentworth, who, along with the Arch-Bishop, that the Scots wanted to see tried.

At first the trial did not go Parliament's way, the available evidence being inconclusive. They, therefore, changed their tactics and instituted something called an 'act of attainment'. This required only a body of suspicious evidence in order to secure a conviction. The problem was that the act required the king's signature. At first he refused to sign.

In an act of extraordinary courage, Wentworth, fearing that his acquital would lead to riots and unnecessary bloodshed, wrote to the king begging him to sign, concluding with this sentence: "To set Your Majesties (sic) Conscience at liberty, I do most humbly beseech Your Majesty for prevention of evils, which may happen by Your refusal, to pass this Bill."[2]

In Ireland, the Catholics and the native clansmen began to fear the prospect of domination by the Protestant New English and Scots Presbyterians. They staged a rebellion, making the spurious claim they were supporting the king. Exaggerated tales of massacres of Protestants by Catholics in Ireland, not all of them erroneous, reached England. This did the king no favours and the stage was set for a revolution in England.

A long and bloody civil war followed in which reprisals by Protestants against Catholics were most bloody in Ireland. As usual, the war was accompanied by disease and famine among the civilian population. At least half a million people died in the conflict, more than half of them in Ireland.

The man who became leader of the Protestant 'New Model Army', Oliver Cromwell, earned a reputation in Ireland as the person responsible for brutal massacres, especially at Drogheda and Wexford. He was, however, a devoutly religious man who believed that Roman Catholicism was an evil subversion of true Christianity. He earnestly believed that it was his mission to execute 'God's design for the nation'. That design, he believed, included 'the free and uninterrupted Passage of the Gospel running through the midst of us' with people free to 'practice and exercise the Faith of the Gospel and lead quiet and peaceable lives in all Godliness and Honesty.'[3] A wish that most Catholics view with distaste and disbelief given his behaviour towards them.

Under his regime, after he became 'Lord Protector' in 1653, there were mass confiscations of lands owned by Catholics. Over 12,000 veterans of the New Model Army were given land in Ireland. Some sold it on to existing Protestant occupiers but around 10,000 remained. Most were single men many of whom, in due course, married Catholic Irish women although such marriages were declared illegal.

In addition, thousands of Scottish covenanter soldiers, who had supported the Parliamentarians, remained in Ulster. Around 12,000 Irish people were sold into servitude in Barbados.

And there were more religious wars to come. The monarchy was restored in 1660 in the shape of Charles II. On his death the crown passed to his brother, James (I of England, VI of

Scotland), a Catholic. And when James's Catholic wife gave birth to a son there was consternation among the Protestants in parliament. They could barely tolerate James's Catholicism. Their hopes had been pinned on James's daughter, Mary, who was married to Charles II's Protestant nephew, William of Orange. James was not expected to live long. That he had produced a son late in life, baptised with Roman rites, appeared to thwart those hopes.

Religious wars had continued on mainland Europe and included an attempted invasion of Protestant Holland by Catholic France which William had successfully repelled. Those in England opposed to the idea of a Catholic succession set about encouraging William to invade. William landed in Devon in November 1688. He and Mary were declared joint sovereigns in February 1689, their coronation taking place two months later. Meanwhile, James had responded by landing in Ireland accompanied by 20,000 French troops. Tens of thousands of Irish Catholics joined them.

The decisive battle that established William and Mary's position as rulers of the archipelago took place 20 miles north of Dublin, in June 1690, when the two armies faced each other across the river Boyne. William's was a multinational force containing Danes and Germans as well as Dutch, Huguenots and English. It was funded by international finance, Portugese Jews and Huguenots. A surprising supporter of William's campaign was the Pope. He feared that a win for James and his French allies would strengthen France's domination of Europe. But it was William's command of strategy that won the day. James went into exile as a guest of the king of France. Pontifical High Mass was held in Rome to celebrate the victory. And the scene was set in Ireland for three centuries of religious conflict based on a myth. In the words of James Connolly: "neither army had the slightest claim to be considered as a patriot army combating for the freedom of the Irish race."[4]

Chapter 3 - Physical Geography

The preceding two chapters sought to provide a broad outline of the historical developments that shaped the relationship between Ireland and its larger neighbour, producing a situation in which ownership of the land was determined by the English ruling class. We now turn to the nature of that land and the reasons for its attractiveness to settlers.

An English man or woman driving around Ireland today, almost anywhere east of the river Shannon, will be struck more by similarities in the landscape than by any differences from their home nation. The central plain and much of the eastern seaboard, through Leinster and into north Munster, is characterised by low, wooded hills, fields of grain and other familiar crops in the valleys; meadows with cattle grazing contentedly on the higher ground. It is a region of fertile river valleys, farm buildings, villages and market towns.

Ireland is well known internationally for its beef and dairy production and its brewing and whiskey distilling tradition. Artisan breads, beers and cheeses are to be found in specialist shops and markets everywhere, as are jams and preserves. The government's food quality assurance agency, Bord Bia, certifies such products as having been produced to the highest possible standards.

According to Bord Bia, whilst wheat for bread baking and barley for malting are grown in significant quantities, only 8% of agricultural land is used to grow commercial crops, including fruit and horticulture. Half of that is devoted to barley. The remaining 92% of all agricultural land is grazing, hay, and silage production, supporting the massive beef and dairy sectors.

Total agricultural production in 2014 was worth €7 billion, about 7.6% of the economy. Irish food accounted for 12.3% of all exports at €11.15 billion*[1] in 2016. €2.4 billion of that was accounted for by 534,000 tonnes of beef and €3.38 billion by dairy products and ingredients. The principal export markets were UK (37%) and the rest of Europe (32%)[1].

This modern pattern of agricultural production is, perhaps surprisingly, not too different from the past. Certainly it is the case that, in the period immediately preceding the famine, cattle and grain were regularly exported to England. The beneficiaries of this trade were not the tenant farmers who produced it, but the landowners and merchants. What angers and frustrates many Irish people is the fact that this pattern of production and trade continued throughout the famine years.

Once our traveller crosses the Shannon he or she will immediately notice a marked difference in the landscape. Fewer hedges and trees are evident, field boundaries being generally

---

1   *The explanation for the value of exports exceeding the value of total production lies in the added value imparted to exported goods, especially dairy, by processing within Ireland.

marked by dry-stone walls and barbed wire. Soon this landscape, too, gives way to a much more mountainous region. The same is generally true of that part of Ireland – West Cork and Kerry – south of the Shannon estuary and west of a line running south from Limerick.

The island of Ireland has been likened to a bowl, the coastal regions generally consisting of mountains, the central plain comparatively flat. That is to ignore the older, lower, mountain ranges, like the Slieve Blooms that mark the centre of the island. The coastal mountain ranges are much more extensive in the west, from the extreme south-west to the far north-west.

To the stranger this landscape appears both beautiful and inhospitable: ideal, perhaps, for a summer holiday enjoying walking, fishing and surfing, but unsuited to daily living throughout the year. Frequent rainstorms may offer a bracing challenge for a fit young person suitably clothed; as an environment in which to attempt to make a living from the land it requires a hardiness of body and spirit that is entirely alien to our modern desk-bound lives.

Yet it is here that the native Irish lived out their lives, herding cattle, growing oats, manufacturing their own clothing by spinning and weaving wool from their sheep, and tanning hides.

Prior to the arrival of the Normans, there was a long tradition of cattle stealing as part of the warfare that manifested itself in constant battles for supremacy between clan leaders.

This tradition continued long after the presence of Anglo-Norman settlers introduced farming methods more like those in use in England. Such methods were unsuited to the rugged land of the west, however, and the Irish continued their traditional pattern of agriculture despite the added burden of having to pay an absent landlord for the right to do so. That right, to occupy the land, was traditionally passed from father to son. If more than one son survived into adulthood the land would be sub-divided unless a marriage could be arranged with the daughter of a neighbour with land to spare. Disputes between clans, and attempted truces, centred on such relationships.

Another important tradition, one that dated back to the establishment of the Church of Rome in these islands, is that of 'Tithing'. One tenth of all food production, or an equivalent in gold or other forms of sponsorship, was given to the Church to provide the personnel and infrastructure needed to maintain the Church and its mission. Sons who chose the Priesthood would not need to inherit a portion of the family land.

In addition there were, especially after the arrival of the Anglo-Normans, frequent calls to furnish man-power and other supplies, or the equivalent in gold, to finance military campaigns such as the Crusades and the frequent wars against Scotland, France and Spain to which brief reference was made in the preceding chapters.

One other geographical feature distinguishes Ireland from its neighbour: the peat bogs. These are most extensive in the west but can be found right across the country. Country dwellers annually harvest peat for their own use for heating their homes. Others use commercially produced peat brickettes. The use of peat in horticulture, actively discouraged in the UK, is still common in Ireland. There are still 3 power stations fuelled by peat, although their future is, at the time of writing, under threat. Their retention depends upon conversion to bio-mass, a process already underway using imported wood waste. Longer term it is hoped to produce sufficient volumes of home grown bio-mass.

The important fact about peat, from the point of view of food production, is that it is acidic and needs the addition of a source of lime in order to make it suitable for the cultivation of more than a narrow range of crops. Traditionally this was achieved, in the west of Ireland, by the use of seaweed and/or crushed sea shells. In the rest of the country limestone was quarried from the hillsides and burned in kilns fuelled by wood or peat. The use of lime for agricultural purposes was probably introduced by the Normans in the 12th century. By the middle of the 17th century its use was widespread.

In England and Wales prior to the eighteenth century, and elsewhere in Europe for another hundred years, agricultural land was organised on the basis of open fields. These were divided into strips each strip belonging to a different member of the community and each growing a different crop so that crops could be rotated to prevent exhaustion of the soil. Beyond the open field was common land where everyone could forage for wild food, for firewood and to graze sheep and cattle. At the centre of such communities was a manor house and church building, surrounded by the cottages occupied by the owners of the strips. In addition to submitting a tithe to the Church, each strip owner had to submit a part of his produce to the Lord of the manor. He, in turn, submitted rent to the member of the aristocracy who was the true owner of the estate on which the village – and many others – was located.

The greatest source of wealth in England from medieval times was wool. Initially wool was sold to weavers on mainland Europe. Later, cloth production in England increased so that it was cloth rather than raw wool that was exported. In order to increase the volume of wool and cloth that was produced it was necessary for two things to happen: more people had to be employed in cloth production instead of subsistence farming, and more land had to be devoted to the grazing of sheep. This was accomplished by a process of enclosing previously common land. Often unpopular, the source of conflict between peasants and aristocracy, the process began in Tudor times and accelerated under various parliamentary acts throughout the 18th century. At the end of the process the land had assumed the patterns familiar today: individual farms dedicated to efficient food production with sheep reared on high pastures in the more mountainous regions.

As the process progressed, food production increased. The discovery and use of various fertilisers played an important part in this increase. The population increased, too, and at a faster rate. The industrial revolution, which enabled the increase in cloth production and the mechanisation of agriculture and transportation, ensured the rapid growth of large centres of population but did not end the poverty that was endemic in the old subsistence farming method. It seemed that the production of food could never keep up with the increase in population. A man called Thomas Malthus developed a theory about this.

So did Adam Smith who also pointed out that this process of privatisation of land ensured that the decreasing number of people occupying land nevertheless received an increasing share of the value produced from the land. It was the aristocratic owners of landed estates who benefited most through the rents charged to farmers and through their control of the manufacturing processes which soon included machinery as well as cloth and other commodities, including the very fertilisers used in food production.

In Ireland some of these developments were introduced by the same aristocratic land-owners, enabling increased production of grain, much of it used to make good the shortfall in production on the mainland. Grain was imported from North America as well. This tended to lower prices so the land-owners successfully lobbied parliament to introduce tariffs – the so called Corn Laws. As parliament consisted largely of the same land-owners, this was not difficult.

Meanwhile in the west of Ireland life continued much as

before. The Irish equivalent to the open field system of subsistence farming is called *rundale*. The people resided in a cluster of homes called a *clachan*. The adjacent land radiated out from the cluster and was farmed communally. The right to grow crops on individual plots rotated among the members so that each had the opportunity to use the best land. In some such communities plots were re-assigned every 3 or 4 years by the casting of lots.

In most *clachan*'s the homes were rudimentary, often consisting of mud walls surrounding a single small room with a turf roof and bare floor. There was very little in the way of furniture. People slept on the floor on straw pallets.

The arrival of the potato changed this pattern. The potato is a highly nutritious food that is easy to grow on poor soil so long as manure and/or seaweed is available to feed the plants. Such reliance on a single crop is, however, dangerous. There were failures of the crop in some years before 1845. The famines that accompanied such failures were short-lived because potatoes were grown in sufficient quantities the next year.

There is a 2-3 month gap between the exhaustion of one year's stock of stored potatoes and the time to harvest the next year's crop. This period, lasting roughly from early June to July/August, saw many people having to rely on whatever they could glean by foraging in the countryside. Those who had cash available could purchase imported maize. Some families pawned their winter clothes in order to raise the necessary cash. At this time of year there was little work to be had on Irish farms. Some men were able to find work on English farms at this time, leaving their women and children to a summer of hunger.

There is ample evidence, however, that the prominence of the potato in the Irish diet ensured that the Irish were generally fitter and stronger than their English counterparts. Studies have found, for example, that Irish men were taller than their English counterparts. They also lived longer than most other Europeans.

In all parts of Ireland people generally married at a younger age than did the English. One benefit of a nutritious diet is the increased survival rate of infants. The population of Ireland generally increased at about the same rate as on the mainland. But there was a far greater increase in the north and west – the very areas that were most dependent on the potato.

Moreover, whereas English peasants displaced from the land could seek opportunities in the rapidly growing industrial towns and cities, no such opportunity existed for the Irish, unless they migrated across the Irish Sea to those same cities, as many did. On the contrary, the mass production of cheap cloth in the Mills of Yorkshire and Lancashire displaced cloth produced by small family weavers in Ireland. Unlike the price protection offered to farmers for their corn, there was no such support for cottage industries in either England or Ireland.

The aristocratic land-owners, however, showed no inclination to follow the pattern of enclosing land. Indeed, they often took little interest in their Irish holdings, leaving decisions in the hands of agents whose principal task was to collect rents. The pattern of continually sub-dividing land continued as the population increased. Many peasants in the lowland areas were permitted to occupy small plots of land on which they grew potatoes. They provided labour to the larger tenant farmers at busy times of year, enabling them to pay rent and buy seed.

Chapter 4 – Economic Geography.

The export of food and other produce requires ready access to sea ports. This, in turn, requires an inland transport infrastructure. As will be seen in later chapters, the major cities and population centres of Ireland developed around ports. Detailed accounts of the development of Dublin, Belfast, Cork and Limerick in the two centuries preceding the famine will be found in Chapter 5. Derry City, Drogheda, Dundalk and Waterford are also ports that form historically important centres of population growth based on international commerce.

In his book *Ireland 1800-1850*, the historian Desmond Keenan defines three types of economy practiced in Ireland in those years[1]. Firstly, the commercial economy, generally centred around these ports and covering their hinterlands up to 30 or so miles inland. Secondly the subsistence economy characterised by "a reasonably abundant production of the necessaries of life, rough clothing, plain food, abundant but poor quality whiskey and beer, rough furniture, adequate but poorly finished housing." Third comes "the cottier economy ... to be found in the remoter parts of the west and south especially where subdivision of property was unchecked."

The first consisted of the production and export of crops

such as wheat, flax, salted butter, wool and leather and the import of fuel, timber, raw sugar, wines, spirits and tobacco, and manufactured goods. Cash and credit were used resulting in the creation of a prosperous merchant class who were able to support the construction of magnificent town houses and spectacular country mansions.

In the second, found most commonly in the Midlands, markets were less well developed. Local brewers and millers purchased and processed the grain produced on small- to medium-sized farms. As the transport infrastructure was developed, with canals, metalled roads and, from the 1830s onward, the railways, so the boundary between the first and second extended inland and became blurred. The live export of cattle was feasible only if the animals were driven from these inland farms to holdings close to the ports were they could be fattened.

Life for the cottiers was reduced to the barest essentials. They tended to marry very young and parents and neighbours would construct a rough cabin for the newlyweds who would then share the land with the parents, unless they were able to reclaim an adjacent area of bog. In Keenan's words, "Few attempts were made to improve (or even clean) the dwellings which resulted in accusations of laziness being made." In a later chapter we shall explore a possible scientific explanation for this lassitude.

Whilst cottiers were to be found in all parts of Ireland, it was only in the west and south-west that they formed the bulk of the population. Travellers were often astonished by the open display of such abject poverty but, so long as the potato lasted the population seemed contented. They have acquired a significance in the mythology of the famine in some quarters, but it would be wrong to suppose that they were typical of pre-Famine Ireland.

It would be wrong, too, to suppose that economic development was confined to the coastal ports. There were significant centres of trade inland also, with an important wool market in Mulingar and Sheep markets in Balinasloe. As trade continued to develop in the early years of the nineteenth century other towns saw growth in prosperity and some hamlets became towns. Despite – arguably because of – the increase in population, gross domestic product increased at a faster rate. Standards of living increased everywhere except among the cottiers where the subdivision of land to provide homes for young couples continued unabated.

Counties Limerick and Clare, home to Mary Marrinan and her landlord Colonel Vandeleur, were the worst affected by such congestion, leading to intense pressure from such men as Vandeleur and Francis Spaight, to encourage emigration in order to clear the land and introduce more efficient forms of cultivation. Francis Spaight became notorious during the famine for welcoming the failure of the potato crop.

A long-time advocate of emigration he appears to have

made the claim, at the height of the famine, *"the failure of the potato crop [is] the greatest possible value in one respect in enabling us to carry out the emigration system."* [2]. As the owner of at least half a dozen emigrant ships it was very much in his interest to maintain the transatlantic traffic on which he depended, bringing cargoes of timber from North America and transporting human cargoes in inadequate accommodation on the return leg.

The name Francis Spaight is notorious for another reason. One of his ships that bore his name was struck by a storm in December 1835. She had sailed from New Brunswick on 25th November. The storm struck on the night of 3rd Of December. Lloyds Register records that at least 20 vessels came to grief that night. The Francis Spaight hove to in order to ride out the storm. Nevertheless she was upended. Four members of the crew were lost overboard, along with most of her provisions. Thirteen of the fifteen remaining crew members survived until discovered by a US registered brig *Angenora* on 23 December.

One can only begin to imagine the parlous state of those men and boys after almost three weeks at sea in mid-winter without food and having only such water as they were able to collect from rainfall. What makes the story notorious is the fact that they had resorted to cannibalism in their desperation, a member of the *Angenora*'s crew stating that on the 18th December, "when finding it impossible to sustain themselves any longer without food, they came to the dreadful resolution of drawing lots which should be killed to sustain the survivors. One poor fellow was eventually killed, and the survivors fed on him until the 20th, when another became deranged and he shared the same fate on the 22nd."[3]

Chapter 5 - The Growth of Cities.

It is worth pausing for a moment to remind ourselves that in the eighteenth century Dublin was a prosperous, cultured city on a par with the greatest cities of Europe. Handel's Messiah had its premier there in 1765. Belfast, Cork and Limerick, too, prospered from the trade that was handled by their ports.

It was during the eighteenth century that Dublin was transformed from a medieval city, with narrow cobbled streets, into a Georgian metropolis with broad boulevards and Palladian buildings. The squares we see today were created then. The landowners referred to in the previous chapter built second homes here. The Lord Lieutenant, Lord Kildare, who already had one of the grandest of the many country houses in Carton House, built the Palladian mansion that today houses the Irish parliament.

When parliament was sitting, in Dublin Castle, the magnates of the Protestant ascendancy arrived with their retinues. Alongside the conducting of government business they staged great banquets and supported, by their patronage, the creative arts of one of the most vibrant and populous cities in the British Empire. All that came to an end with the Act of Union. Now there was no longer a parliament to attend; no need for that second home, however grand.

Meanwhile the outer parts of the city remained undeveloped. A steady migration of mainly Catholic families from the surrounding countryside both created slums in which rival gangs vied for supremacy, and ensured that Catholics were in the majority by the end of the century. With the ending of the Parliamentary 'season', many of the city's once elegant Georgian neighbourhoods rapidly became slums, too.

By the 1840s, the emancipation of the Roman Catholic population produced a situation in which the City Corporation became dominated by Catholics, among them Daniel O'Connell who, whilst campaigning for repeal of the Act, became mayor.

***

Whilst Dublin's prosperity was built on the patronage of high society, Belfast thrived as a merchant town and the centre of industry. It was the only part of Ireland to benefit from the Industrial Revolution. It did see similar, but smaller scale, developments of Georgian streets and buildings. In the early years of the nineteenth century, it also saw a similar inward migration of mainly Catholic families from the rural hinterland although this was eclipsed by migration from Scotland, England and further afield in Ireland.

Towards the end of the eighteenth century the first Roman Catholic Church building in Belfast was funded by protestant business men and Church of Ireland and Presbyterian congregations. A largely Presbyterian military guard of honour was provided for the parish priest on the occasion of the first mass celebrated there on the 30th May 1784.

***

Cork benefited enormously from wars during the eighteenth century. First the American War of Independence, then the Napoleonic wars, saw the port as a principal provisioning centre for the Royal Navy. It was also a centre for the export of food to mainland Britain and to the West Indies. Butter, salt beef and pork featured heavily. The Cork butter market, with its rigorously enforced quality system, became the largest and most well known such facility in Europe.

Tanning, brewing, distilling and textiles were also important to the growth of Cork throughout the eighteenth century. Linen for sails, wool and cotton for uniforms and civilian clothing, and beer, gin and whiskey were all exported from the port.

Hand in hand with the growth of the economy went a steady development of the physical infrastructure with the reclamation of several marshes and the creation of the street layout familiar to visitors today, including several bridges across the river Lee.

The ending of the Napoleonic Wars in 1815 reduced the need to service the Royal Navy. Demand for food fell, too, with a corresponding fall in prices. There were always high levels of unemployment in the city, despite the growth of trade, with a steady influx of poor people from the rural hinterland and further afield. With the collapse of the city's economy in the 1820s, unemployment rose to very high levels. In 1832 there was a Europe wide cholera epidemic which further depressed economic conditions.

Shipbuilding, brewing, distilling, tanning and the butter trade still flourished and Cork Harbour remained a major port for trans-Atlantic trade. However, these were not sufficient to reduce the high levels of unemployment that served to depress wages and contributed to the poor living conditions in the densely populated inner city.

As in Dublin, Catholic emancipation in the 1800s led to the substitution of the ruling Protestant elite on the City Corporation with a majority drawn from the Catholic merchant class.

***

Like Cork, Limerick benefited from the trans-Atlantic trade. In the second half of the eighteenth century a new city was constructed to the south of the original medieval city, with wide streets and fine Georgian terraced houses. Some of Ireland's finest examples of Georgian Architecture can be seen at the Crescent area and Pery Square.

Chief imports through the port included timber, coal, iron

and tar. Exports included beef, pork, wheat, oats, flour and emigrants bound for North America.

One of the great exponents of emigration, with the declared intention of clearing his estates of 'paupers' was Francis Spaight. He ordered the construction of a small fleet of ships specifically for the purpose and advertised sailings each spring in the decade preceding the onset of the Great Famine. Other owners of large estates close to Limerick who advocated and encouraged emigration included the Vandeleur family.

As noted in the preceding chapter, many other towns saw expansion in this period, often financed and encouraged by Protestant ascendancy landowners. One such was the small port of Kilrush on the northern bank of the Shannon estuary. The Vandeleur family established the town, building many grand town houses and encouraging merchants and professional people to become established in the town. The town's layout with broad streets named after family members, when seen today, suggests a degree of self confidence verging on arrogance. As in Belfast, and no doubt many other places, it was the Protestants, in this case the Vandeleur family, who provided the land and some of the funding, for the building of an imposing Roman Catholic church and, after the famine, a Convent for the Sisters of Mercy.

And yet, despite this apparent philanthropy, the Vandeleurs also became notorious for mass evictions of tenants and cottiers from their land. And despite the prosperity that enabled the creation of those streets and buildings, Kilrush was, by 1847, declared to be one of the 20 most distressed of 130 Irish Poor Law Unions.

Chapter 6 – "Top Dog" Mentality

For more than two hundred years British explorers and traders had travelled the world, discovering new lands bordering the Pacific and Indian Oceans. They developed trade links with the indigenous populations of these lands and profited enormously from that trade. They were not alone. Dutch, French, Spanish and Portugese merchants and adventurers were doing the same. Conflicts often ensued, engendering frequent wars. Britain usually came out on top and, by the beginning of the nineteenth century, large parts of Africa as well as the Indian sub-continent, all of Australia, New Zealand, many Pacific Islands, southern China and most of North America were governed by the British monarchy or its authorised agents.

The oldest of these colonies, those on the eastern seaboard of North America, had formed themselves into the United States of America, fought for and won independence. But there were many other lands that offered opportunities for those seeking adventure.

At the same time it could be said that Britain was leading the way in scientific advancement. Some of those early explorers, such as James Cook, had pioneered techniques of surveying and map making as well as bringing back numerous geological and botanical specimens to add to the world's fund of knowledge. Others had developed, and conducted experiments to prove, scientific theories that formed the basis of our modern understanding of chemistry, physics, astronomy and medicine.

Little wonder, then, that they regarded themselves, their beliefs and their systems of government to be superior to any others. In particular, the old ideas embodied by the Roman Catholic Church were deemed to be barely superior to the pagan practices and idolatry of the natives of Africa, the Far East and North America who had proved so easy to exploit. If certain among the Irish chose to cling to such outdated notions, if those same people were also poor and ignorant, then must there not be a causal link between the two? All that was necessary for the Irish to escape from their fate was for them to acquire the enlightened Protestant education that had produced the scholars, sailors and merchants that had made the acquisition of such an empire possible.

It was certainly the case that many of these colonies needed labour. They especially needed people who were capable of taking undeveloped land and turning it into productive farmland. Successful farmers from across the British Isles were, therefore, encouraged to emigrate to the colonies. And individuals who chose to defy the law could be sent as punishment to work as slave labour.

Many Irish Protestants joined in these empire building enterprises, serving in the British army and navy and as crewmen on privately operated cargo vessels. Catholics were prevented by law from entering the army and many other professions. Many of them therefore studied overseas and served in the armies of Britain's enemies: France, Spain, Portugal and the Austro-Hungarian Empire. A member of at least one comparatively wealthy Catholic family, that of which Daniel O'Connell was a scion, became a general in Empress Marie-Therese's army and was awarded a baronetcy by her.

Irish men and women of both religious persuasions sought the opportunities presented by the ready availability of land in these new surroundings. Meanwhile in Ireland the practice of sub-dividing land to provide for a rapidly increasing population continued, despite the incentives offered by some landlords to encourage such migration.

Educated Britons did not stop at developing and testing scientific theories. They concerned themselves with philosophical and social problems, especially those associated with the increasing population and the poverty that seemed inevitably to accompany it. How was it possible to ensure that the production of food kept pace with the growing number of mouths to feed? As the industrial revolution progressed and more people left the countryside for over-crowded cities, the old pattern of living, in which food was transported over relatively short distances to markets close to where people lived, was superseded by new modes of transport. Canals, railways and metalled roads made it possible to transport food from the fields to markets in the burgeoning centres of manufacturing.

A new field of study opened up as scholars attempted to understand the increasingly complex relationship between production and consumption and the problem of ensuring that workers, who no longer had access to the possibility of growing even some of their own food, were able to earn enough from their new activities, operating machinery, to provide the basic necessities of life.

How to share the wealth produced by the activities of merchant explorers and, later, by machines, among the whole population, instead of enriching a few whilst the majority struggled in conditions of abject poverty? As we have seen, men like Adam Smith pointed out that rent placed an added, unfair, burden on wealth creators[1]. Others speculated about the relationship between increases in food production and the growth in population. On the one hand the more people were employed in all kinds of production, the more that could be produced. On the other, the more food that was available, the longer people tended to live, especially young people. Whereas it was, in the past, not uncommon for children to die from any of a variety of diseases before reaching puberty, the more well fed they were the more likely they were to survive into adulthood and become parents themselves. Was there a limit on the ability of the available land to produce sufficient food?

Whilst new lands were available for food production in the colonies, the cost of transporting this food across the ocean was considerable. In the view of some it made more sense to take the people to the food, rather than bring the food to the people. This, then, was another reason to encourage people to emigrate. A reason, too, to remove from the British Isles those individuals whom the authorities deemed to be undesirable.

As mentioned in chapter 3, one of the thinkers of the period, Thomas Malthus, examined the evidence and concluded that there was, indeed, a limit to the food production capacity of the land[2]. The population had consistently grown at a faster rate than had the volume of food production. It was, he insisted, necessary to take steps to limit the growth of population, especially among the very poor. If they produced fewer children it would be easier to ensure that those children were well fed and housed to an acceptable standard. It might even be possible to end the practice of sending children out to work at a very young age. They could be sent, instead, to school where education would fit them for a better life.

Meanwhile, the very uneven distribution of wealth enabled those with vast amounts of it to indulge themselves by building large houses with productive walled gardens and landscaped parkland covering several hundred acres. The houses were filled with artifacts brought from all around the world. They planted the parklands with species of trees and shrubs, the seeds of which were also brought from distant lands. This happened across Ireland as well as England, Scotland and Wales. Many of the owners of these houses built towns to house the people who worked in the house and on the estate. Few were inclined to sully the beautiful landscape within which they had carefully chosen to build by introducing modern industries to provide alternative employment for their tenants.

The tenants were content – they had a house with a plot on which to grow their potatoes. Sometimes, sufficient space to permit someone else to grow potatoes, too. If that person built a rough cabin on the plot and took up residence, so much the better. The rent he paid helped ensure there was enough seed for next year.

But, to make the estate profitable and ensure that the landowner had the means to pay the large retinue of servants and gardeners, he needed the tenants of the estate's farms to produce the kind of food that could easily be exported to the industrial centres of England where the growing population was a source of increasing demand. Growing more food for export required a more efficient use of the land. Too many tenants of larger holdings had allowed labourers, most of whom worked only at those times of year when there was high demand for farm labour, to set up home in cabins, each with its own potato patch. That space could be better utilised to graze cattle or grow wheat or barley.

Many landlords therefore embarked upon a policy of encouraging and providing limited assistance for emigration. When that failed they turned to the mass eviction of tenants. None had anything that would be recognised today as security of tenure. Had they done so, they would not have had the necessary resources to pursue a case at law.

Not all landlords thought along these lines. A few did facilitate the development of 'ideal' industrial towns on their estates. One such was at Portlaw, in County Waterford, where a Quaker family established a successful cotton mill. Portlaw is the only community in Ireland whose population increased during the famine years.

Many of those who owned large estates in Ireland rarely visited them. They left them in the care of agents, many of whom were content to pocket the small rents paid by the labourers and small subsistence farmers. Pressure to change came from government, members of which, perhaps heeding the messages of men like Malthus, wanted to maximise the production of food for the masses congregating in expanding cities like Liverpool, Birmingham and Manchester, as well as the capital. For their part, the landowners were concerned about competition from such food as could be imported easily from the colonies, notably American grain. As already noted, they lobbied for, and got, the application of tariffs on foreign grain.

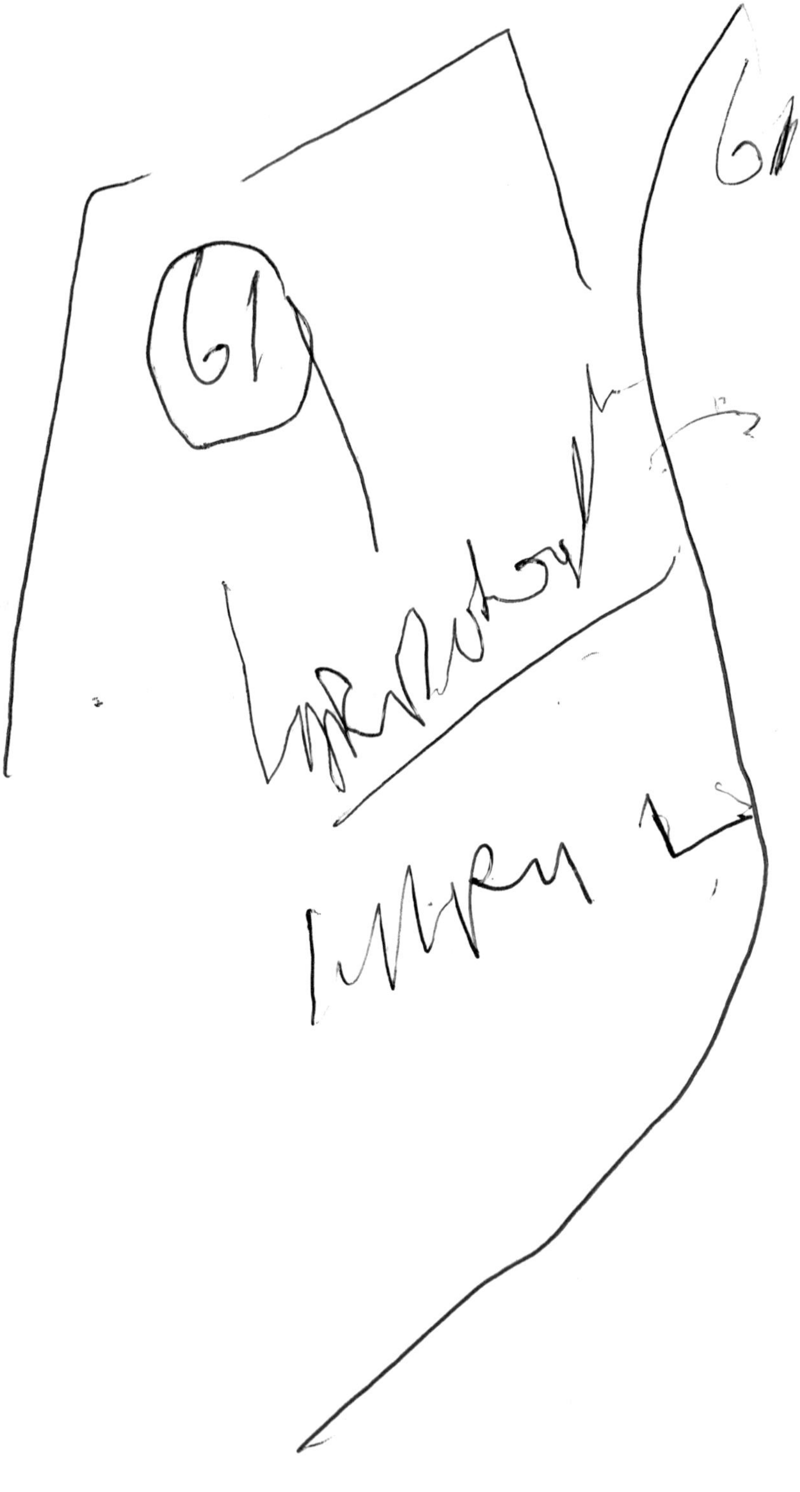
G1

Chapter 7 - Responding to Poverty

Anyone whose education included the most rudimentary study of the Christian bible will be familiar with Jesus of Nazareth's remark that the poor will always be with us. A study of history similarly demonstrates that poverty has existed throughout the ages, a condition that seems to resist all attempts at a remedy. Is this failure to eliminate the condition inevitable, or is it, rather, the consequence of the inadequacy of the measures taken to alleviate it?

For the purpose of this book we need not look back over 2000 years of history. It will suffice to examine only the period we have already explored in terms of the struggles over land ownership and religious belief outlined in the first two chapters. Prior to the reformation – the switch, over large parts of Europe, from Roman Catholicism to Protestantism – the poor were looked after by the monasteries. The funding for this came from the patronage the monasteries received from the landowners and from the tithes paid by farmers. Whilst the old, the sick and the disabled were provided with food, shelter and healing, the able bodied were provided with work, either in farms that formed an important part of the religious community or on building construction and maintenance.

For the able bodied individual who could not find work near his place of abode the only alternative was to travel to a place where there was work available. Others might travel from place to place plying a particular trade, or offering a service, moving on when the demand for the service in that area had been satisfied.

Throughout this period there were years when crops failed causing famine. Epidemics of disease occurred from time to time. The 'Black Death', the plague that devastated Europe in the 14th century, for example, reduced the population by 30%. Wars, too, took their toll on populations, although they also provided a source of income for those who chose, or were forced, to join one or other of the many armies and navies that took part. With the men away fighting, the bulk of the labour necessary to grow food fell to the women and children. Wars were often responsible for the failure of crops. As we have seen, this was sometimes a deliberate act of destruction, perpetrated as part of the campaign. At others it was the consequence of the absence of farm labourers, meaning that insufficient crops were sown.

The destruction of the monasteries meant they were no longer able to carry on the work of alleviating poverty. In Britain, it now fell to the Parishes to administer poor relief under the first of a string of 'poor laws' that were introduced and amended throughout the 16th and 17th centuries. In order to qualify for relief you had to be able to prove a connection to the parish from which you were claiming. If you were a stranger, you would need to travel to the parish where you were born or where you could demonstrate a long term affinity. Such relief, when applied to individuals deemed capable of work, was conditional upon the individual undertaking some form of work in return. It was funded by levying a rate (property tax based on the notional value of the property) on the landowners of the parish.

By the 18th century this idea, that assistance must be earned by performing work, had become well established. After all, someone else's labour had created the food, clothing and shelter with which you were being provided. It was only right that you should perform some service in return.

For those not completely indigent, survival depended on payment received in return for their labour, whether as agricultural labourers or in the factories appearing in the growing industrial centres. The balance between wages and the price of food and other necessities became an important factor influencing the extent of poverty.

The practical manifestation of the principle of work in return for relief for the indigent was the workhouse. The first of these was established in Bristol at the end of the 17th century. The movement grew throughout the 18th century as the larger parishes, and groups of small parishes, set up similar institutions. By 1776 there were over 1900 such institutions in England and Wales, housing an estimated 100,000 individuals, most of them children, sick or elderly.

The Dublin House of Industry was established in 1772 to care for vagrants and beggars. In times of more general distress the work of this and similar institutions in other cities was supplemented by *ad hoc* provision by the parishes raising funds by subscription. Reading accounts of the conditions that prevailed in the early 1780s, for example, it is clear that the response to widespread food and fuel shortages that occurred then consisted of a combination of fire-fighting with limited financial resources and attempts by the government in Dublin to control markets and prices. Such attempts were actively opposed by merchants who often combined to frustrate philanthropic actions such as the donation of 2000 tons of free coal from the mine owner Sir James Lowther.

In addition to fund raising appeals by the parishes and government's attempts to control markets and prices, some landlords offered alternative employment to workers displaced by such events as the failure of the flax crop in 1782 that left weavers unable to ply their trade. In rural areas many communities took the law into their own hands, waylaying cartloads of grain destined for the cities.

According to James Kelly, "Acts of benevolence by landlords and clergy, and donations to institutions like the Houses of Industry, were vital for the control of distress in late eighteenth century Ireland. ... In Dublin the House of Industry was the most important agent of relief, but it worked with local committees and was heavily reliant on donations.... while in the countryside landlords, wealthy farmers and clergy were indispensable."[1]

Note, however, that whereas there were numerous workhouses in England and Wales there were only a handful in Ireland, even though poverty and famines, or near famines, were much more common there. After the Act of Union at the commencement of the 19th century the government in London considered various ways of tackling this problem which was beginning to affect social cohesion in England. A growing number of poor Irish families were migrating to England. Whilst they were not able to take advantage of the poor relief available there until they had established 5 years residence, their presence was perceived as a threat to both wages and social order.

Education was seen as one important way of ending poverty, by equipping individuals with the skills to enable them to obtain work. During the second half of the 18th century a number of Protestant organisations established schools in Ireland. Catholics had been banned from providing education as part of the policy of suppressing the old religion. Once the ban was lifted, Catholic schools also began to appear. Unlike the Protestant schools, however, these did not receive government support. By the 1830s, the government decided to establish a National school system which would be multi-denominational, run by committees containing both Catholic and Protestant members.

Although this put Ireland ahead of the mainland in terms of state funded education, Ireland was not progressing economically or socially. A number of government initiated surveys and reports were commissioned but their recommendations were generally deemed to be too costly to implement. One such commission, headed by the Protestant archbishop of Dublin, recommended that the poor law, as established in England, would not work in Ireland because of the lack of available work. This conclusion was unacceptable to the authorities in London who sent one of the commissioners responsible for administering the poor law in England to look at the situation in Ireland.

We saw in a previous Chapter how the English regarded themselves as superior to the native populations of the lands they conquered. However well justified this attitude might have seemed given the evident successes achieved by English Soldiers, Seamen and Scientists, it looks today like extreme arrogance. The modern liberal view is that a person's ethnic origin has no bearing on his or her intelligence or ability to acquire useful skills. This was not so in the first half of the nineteenth century. The English establishment viewed the native Irish in exactly the same way as they viewed the natives of Africa.

The remarks of the poor law commissioner, George Nicholls, illustrate this perfectly. "They seem to feel no pride, no emulation; to be heedless of the present, and reckless of the future. They do not ... strive to improve their appearance or add to their comforts. Their cabins still continue slovenly, smoky, filthy, almost without furniture or any article of convenience or decency ... If you point out these circumstances to the peasantry themselves, and endeavour to reason with and show them how easily they might improve their condition and increase their comforts, you are invariably met by excuses as to their poverty ...'Sure how can we help it, we are so poor' ... whilst at the same time (he) is smoking tobacco, and had probably not denied himself the enjoyment of whiskey."[2]

His conclusion was that a new poor law should be enacted for Ireland which should include the provision of a network of 130 workhouses and that these institutions would not be permitted to provide relief other than within their walls. It was felt that this would deter all but those deemed to be the most deserving people from claiming relief. Each workhouse would have space for 800 persons, would be administerd by a Board of Guardians and financed by a local property tax.

It is worth noting, too, that the number of inmates in English workhouses, based on the figures above, was around 50. The fact that a standard capacity of 800 was deemed necessary for Ireland, amounting to over 100,000 total across the 130 unions, speaks volumes about the extent of poverty there in the years immediately preceding the famine. It is also notable that, whereas in England the workhouses were based in existing communities and more or less integrated into the existing administrative framework of local government and law administration, a whole new layer of governance was imposed on Ireland, with each Poor Law Union, together with its workhouse, covering a much wider area so that potential beneficiaries would have to travel long distances in order to receive assistance.

The policy was quickly implemented. When the potato crop failed in the second half of the 1840s each workhouse in this network became the base from which relief would be administered. They would prove to be utterly inadequate to perform the task, although, in fairness to the Boards of Guardians, most did their best with the limited resources available to them.

Chapter 8 – Nutrition and Mental Development

Whilst history, geography, religion and the arrogance of the British aristocracy all played a part in creating the conditions for disaster, there remains an unanswered question at the heart of the story of the famine that devastated Ireland during the years from 1845-52. Why did those who suffered not fight back more vigorously? There certainly were incidents of theft, often punished severely. There were demonstrations outside the premises of merchants. There was a small rebellion by a group calling themselves "Young Ireland", all of whom were comparatively wealthy. But accounts of such incidents are rare when compared to the numerous tales of people dying in their homes, succumbing to a dreadful apathy and resignation.

It was not only during the famine that Irish paupers were observed to be exhibiting such attitudes. The words of George Nicholls, quoted in Chapter 7, were written more than a dozen years before the potato blight struck. Phrases like: "If you ... endeavour to reason with and show them how easily they might improve their condition and increase their comforts, you are invariably met by excuses as to their poverty" are revealing, and not only in the prejudice of the observer that they might indicate.

It is tempting to suggest that religion was to blame for this. The belief that the conditions the people endured were providential, that they were inflicted upon them as punishment for supposed sins, was certainly expressed in many quarters. The notion that prayers could provide the answer to a person's problems, central to both Catholicism and Protestantism, encourages the idea that God will provide. And there is ample evidence that proselytising elements within Protestantism took advantage of the situation to preach the need for conversion to what to them was the "true faith".

It is possible, however, that modern science provides us with a much more rational answer. To fully understand the impact of this it is helpful to recall that famines, or near famines, caused by crop failure, were frequent occurrences in the century or more that preceded the mid-eighteen-hundreds

Whilst there is evidence that the highly nutritious potato diet ensured that young men joining the British armed forces or working on English infrastructure projects were on the whole taller and stronger than their English counterparts, it is not unreasonable to assume that these individuals left Ireland to take up such employment before the annual summer dearth, the period following exhaustion of last year's stock. Those whom they left behind, principally women and children, would have endured 2 to 3 months of near starvation before the new crop was ready to harvest.

Neuroscience is a comparatively modern discipline. Some of its practitioners have carried out studies aimed at identifying the impact of diet and nutrition upon the development of the human brain. These have been mostly aimed at assessing the value of various dietary supplements administered to pregnant women and infants. What they demonstrate *inter alia* is that there is a strong link between inadequate nutrition and impeded pre- and post-natal mental development.

It is, surely, not unreasonable to conclude that any child born during the 'waiting months' of July and August, or one or two months after that, would have his or her mental development impaired as a result of the absence of certain nutrients from their diet, or that of their mother in the final semester of pregnancy.

Furthermore, the periodic famines and food shortages that occurred in the years leading up to the years of potato blight, would suggest that there were many years during which a significant number of births were so affected.

And what, precisely, are those effects? In March 2013 the journal *Frontiers of Neuroscience* published a review of published papers on the subject[1]. Some of the conclusions reached are interesting:

• Since rapid brain growth occurs during the first 2 years of life (and by the age of 2 the brain reaches 80% of its adult weight), this period of life may be particularly sensitive to deficiencies in diet

• studies of infants with vitamin B12 deficiencies reported a variety of abnormal clinical and radiological signs, including: hypotonic muscles, involuntary muscle movements, apathy, cerebral atrophy, and demyelination of nerve cells

• severe iodine deficiency during pregnancy may cause

"cretinism" in children

• most observational studies on iodine deficient children found some degree of cognitive impairment

• malnourished children have less energy and interest for learning that negatively influences cognitive development

• even mild but persistent malnutrition in early life (i.e., during the first 2 years of life) negatively influences reasoning, visuospatial functions, IQ, language development, attention, learning, and academic achievement

What does all this mean? Surely the key point is that, whereas Nicholls and other English officials held the belief that the Irish were responsible for their condition because of an innate indolence and lassitude, the truth is the opposite: it was their condition that caused the observed behavioural deficiencies.

We will probably never know precisely what specific nutrients were absent from the Irish diet at different times. But, given repeated shortages of food over several generations, there can be little doubt that important minerals and/or vitamins were often lacking and that, as a consequence, pregnancies entered into during or shortly before such periods had a high likelihood of producing individuals with less than optimal subsequent mental development.

Part 2 – The Famine Years

Chapter 9 – Autumn-Winter 1845/6

The most remarkable characteristics of potato blight are the speed with which it spreads – via spores borne on the wind – and the equal rapidity with which affected plants are consumed by the pathogen once established. A crop which one day appears perfectly healthy will, within twenty four hours, be blackened and putrid. The progression of this destruction from field to field and from county to county is accomplished in a matter of days.

Because the blight arrived on the east coast of Ireland and progressed westwards, some of the crop in the far west was harvested before the blight reached it. Nevertheless, there was a significant shortage, exacerbated because, before the first appearance of the blight in Ireland, Irish potatoes were exported to Holland and mainland Britain where the blight had struck first. It's also worth recalling that its arrival was preceded by the usual period of inadequate diet that followed the exhaustion of the previous season's crop. A people that were expecting relief from near starvation were, instead, confronted by the prospect of continuing famine.

Those who had pawned their winter clothes to enable them to buy seed and meal now lacked the means to redeem them. They faced a winter not merely of starvation but of bitter cold with inadequate clothing.

The authorities in Ireland and in London responded as

politicians always do: by blaming aspects of government policy which they opposed and asserting that alternative policies they were already advocating would, if in place, have averted the crisis. This centred on the prevailing debate at the time between advocates of free trade on the one hand and protectionism, in the shape of the corn laws, on the other.

In practical terms, two specific remedial measures were introduced. Robert Peel's government authorised the purchase of £100,000 of maize on the New York market which was imported into Ireland to be distributed via depots managed by the Coast Guard. The purpose was not so much to feed the people directly as to interfere in the market, reducing the price of locally produced grain. A consequence that was bitterly resented by the merchants.

The second measure was the institution of a programme of public works, consisting of road building and drain construction. Both of these measures were accompanied by the repeal of the Corn Laws. Neither took effect until the spring of 1846 by which time the distress of the population had begun to manifest itself in food and labour riots.

Proposals, by Daniel O'Connell and others, to introduce a temporary ban on whiskey production and on the export of grain from Ireland were rejected as being unwarranted interference in the market.

Maize proved to be an unpopular food. Despite the distribution of government leaflets instructing recipients on how to make use of it, it became known derogatorily as 'Peel's brimstone', perhaps because the illiteracy of the worst affected individuals meant they were unable to read or comprehend written instructions – and failure to follow instructions for the proper preparation of maize can make it difficult to digest. It was not distributed free of charge. Those unable to pay had either to enrol on a public works scheme or enter the workhouse which necessitated the surrender of whatever meagre possessions they had, including their clothes which were replaced by a rough uniform.

The public works funding was at times misused by landlords, both to undertake work on their own estates and to employ family members and assist their tenants rather than the most needy. When the English press began to pick up on such corruption Peel's government came under attack for being too generous. At the same time, treasury officials, under the leadership of Charles Trevelyan, argued that the landowners should take on a larger burden of responsibility.

In May of 1846 the American teacher, writer and Congregationalist, Asenath Nicholson made her second visit to Ireland where she was to remain for almost 3 years. She travelled extensively and recorded what she witnessed in a book entitled *Lights and Shade of Ireland*. Observing the stark differences between the land owning aristocracy and the poor who laboured for them, she likened the condition of the Irish poor to that of slaves in her native land. They were, she contended, enslaved in their situation, enslaved to their employers, enslaved to the system and, worst of all, enslaved to the potato. If there was idleness – and she was philosophically opposed to idleness – it was to be found in all classes: "the rich are idle from a silly pride and long habits of indulgence; and the poor because no man 'hires them'"

She stressed the fact that the economy of rural Ireland was very different to that of England, the implication being that the approach to the problem of rural poverty embraced by the government in London was inappropriate.

As for that government, by June of 1846 opposition from all sides led to its dissolution. It was replaced by a minority Whig administration under Lord John Russell who was less supportive of Peel's measures. The Relief Commission Peel had created was stood down, the new government responded positively to lobbying by grain merchants by agreeing not to interfere in the market by importing further quantities of maize at government expense. In place of the Commission, the relief effort was entirely in the hands of the Treasury with its determination to make the landowners carry the burden of relief.

Of course, by this time potato plots across Ireland were flourishing and, with the new season's crop in prospect, there was reason for some degree of optimism. Alternative foods would still be needed for some time, alongside the continuing public works programme to provide people with the means to purchase them. However, the public works programme was revamped, with a determination to make the landlords pay and to exclude works of benefit only to landlords. The principle was that employment on such schemes was to be regarded as an absolute last resort. A system of 'payment by measure' was introduced. But malnourished people have a limited capacity for physical labour so that many were unable to earn enough to feed themselves and their families adequately.

Meanwhile the government in London had been grappling for a number of years with the problem of 'encumbered estates'. This was the result of the common practice among Irish landowners of raising mortgages and other charges on their estates in order to indulge a life style that the income from their estates was incapable of sustaining. As Sir James Graham commented in a letter to Peel in September, 1843, "The real secret of the evils of Ireland is the bankrupt condition of the landlords"[2]. Lord Stanley had underlined Graham's point in June, 1845, when he stated that the under-capitalised state of Irish agriculture was the root of Irish discontent. With so much debt it was impossible for estate owners to raise the capital necessary for improvement of their land in order to make it more productive. Part of Peels' rationale for the repeal of the Corn Laws was his belief that it would release capital enabling such improvements. With greater productivity from the land, tenants would be able to pay higher rents increasing the landowners' incomes.

Towards the end of 1845 Lord Devon, who had been

commissioned to investigate the problem and recommend solutions, produced his report. Its principal recommendation was that the law should be changed to permit the sale of such estates, the aim being to allow wealthy merchants to invest in them. The first draft of such a bill was introduced into parliament early in 1846 but lapsed with Peel's resignation in July.

Irish grain merchants imported maize in the summer of 1846 for sale at market prices. But, as fields of bright green studded with star shaped white flowers flourished across the island, thoughts of the autumn's potato harvest must have brought hope to many, both in Ireland and in the British Treasury where there may well have been sighs of relief at the prospect of a crisis averted or, at least, avoided.

Chapter 10 – Autumn-Winter 1846/7

If the idea that the crisis had been averted was indeed harboured in the minds of the people, their landlords, or the officials and politicians charged with the responsibility of handling the crisis, it was to be cruelly destroyed by the reappearance of the blight as July of 1846 came to an end.

The new government, led by Lord John Russell, had Peel's support and that of the less protectionist of his supporters. It consisted of a coalition of interrelated aristocratic families who supported free trade, and radical thinkers, such as middle class manufacturers John Bright and Richard Cobden, alongside utilitarian followers of Bentham, the keenest proponents of limiting and rationalising the state. It also had the support of Irish MPs, including Daniel O'Connell and his followers.

The Benthamites held that it was the relationship of landlord and tenant that lay at the root of Irish economic backwardness. They looked positively on the alternative model of peasant proprietorship existing in other European countries. Once predatory landlordism had been restrained and peasants secured in their holdings, they believed the 'magic of property' would create the necessary motivation for investment and exertion from below. Russell made clear his belief that the cost of relieving the poverty of Irish paupers was to be met by the owners of Irish land. This, despite his being well aware that many lacked the means to do so.

The public works programme was now expanded. Former army officers were recruited alongside engineers to supervise the various programmes. Local relief committees drew up lists of people eligible for employment on the schemes. These lists were vetted by inspectors, supposedly to remove any who might have been placed on the list as a favour to a friend or relative of one or more board members. In practice, such pruning of the lists was entirely arbitrary, some inspectors exercising their powers with the zeal of the worst kind of modern day "jobs worth".

Meanwhile, the conditions under which the works were performed were akin to those of forced labour camps. When one unpopular supervisor in County Clare was shot at and wounded all work on that site was suspended until the perpetrator was apprehended. This left 900 families without the means to purchase fuel or food in what was turning out to be one of the coldest Decembers on record[1].

Such suspensions were in accordance with Board of Works policy. A fortnight after this particular example, the inspector who imposed the suspension reported having witnessed, "crowds of [women and little children] scattered over the turnip fields, like a flock of famished crows, devouring the raw turnips ... shivering in the snow and sleet, [the women] uttering exclamations of despair whilst their children were screaming with hunger"[2]. Nevertheless, a further two weeks passed before the works were reopened. Similar closures occurred throughout the winter in the harshest weather in living memory.

Despite constant culling of names from the work lists, the number of people employed on them grew rapidly, from 100,000 to 700,000 between November 1846 and March 1847. That figure, of 700,000, represents almost one tenth of the total population of the island. Moreover, each was responsible for up to four other family members. As such, it provides a vivid illustration of the extent of the suffering of the people. And it was not uniformly spread across the country. The west fared much worse than elsewhere.

Seamen delivering cargoes of food to ports on the west coast noted the suffering of the people. Their descriptions were published in newspapers and journals in Ireland and in England. One such description talks of famine scenes that are "all alike, getting worse as you go south, and at Schull (in County Cork) and its neighbourhood the very climax of misery finds its resting place."[3] Another, speaking of Ballydehob, a few miles from Schull, reports that "deaths here average 40 or 50 daily ... children of 10 and 9 years old I have mistaken for decrepit old women, their faces wrinkled, their bodies bent and distorted with pain."[4]

These observations were made in February as supplies of food for distribution were delivered to the ports of the west on behalf of the Quakers and in anticipation of the implementation of the Soup Kitchens Act. Meanwhile, demand for work was such that there were labour riots in some places. Men arrived at selection points in their hundreds, sometimes bringing their own spades, hoping to be enlisted on to construction projects.

One can only marvel at the level of bureaucracy required to support such a vast undertaking as the public works scheme employing so many. An army of Engineers, supervisors and inspectors poring over schemes and the work lists, whilst local committees of "the great and the good", landlords, merchants, Catholic priests and Church of Ireland rectors, battled to get those most in need accepted onto the schemes.

Country dwellers were the most affected by the crisis. The relief effort was administered from towns and cities so the destitute country folk made their way to them. At first they were helped by citizens but as time went on, and people began to succumb to diseases like cholera and dysentery, the new arrivals were shunned. Families who previously had taken in desperate strangers now threw them out. In Cork, Father Matthew observed that: *"The citizens are determined to get rid of them. They take up stray beggars and vagrants and confine them at night in the market place, and the next morning send them out in a cart five miles from the town and there they are left and a great part of them perish for they have no home to go to."*[5]

Meanwhile charitable organisations and individuals did what they could. First-hand accounts of the situation began to appear in newspapers and journals on the mainland, especially *The Illustrated London News*. Assorted philanthropists established a British Association for Relief which raised money from Church door collections and organised a "National Day of Fast and Humiliation" on 24th March. The initial response was generous, raising upwards of £435,000 for distribution.

In addition, The Society of Friends raised money in America and Britain and set up the first soup kitchens: places where hot food was prepared and distributed to the destitute. The Society provided practical support as well. They redeemed fishing nets and other essential equipment pawned by desperate fishermen. The coastal waters around Ireland, especially in the west, are not an abundant source of fish, the rocky bottom is not a good feeding ground for fish. Coastal dwellers relied on molluscs and seaweed as sources of food and income. The Quakers funded the purchase of vessels and nets suitable for deep sea fishing and provided training for potential crews. They also played a leading role in the expansion and modernisation of a linen industry.

But it was the government work programme that formed the backbone of relief for the majority of those that qualified. By the spring the Board of Works had expended £5 million. In theory this was supposed to be recovered from Irish landowners through the levying of a rate. Although a proportion of the works undertaken were useful, much was not, just work for work's sake, building roads that led nowhere. What proportion of the £5 million actually ended up in the hands of the hungry and how much went in salaries to the administrators or as payment for tools is hard to uncover.

In March the government in London finally conceded that the policy was failing. Over the succeeding months the works were wound down and a network of soup kitchens established based on the Poor Law Unions. There was, however, a hiatus with many work schemes closing before the alternative food distribution centres were up and running. Nevertheless, around 3 million people received food daily from these public kitchens during the summer of 1847. For the first time imports of grain into Ireland substantially exceeded exports. Grain prices halved between February and August.

Meanwhile the workhouses were filling up, with many building extensions and acquiring buildings for conversion. Fever hospitals, too, were filling up and the numbers of deaths occurring increased steadily through the spring although they fell as more hot food became available via the kitchens. Now, it was not only the destitute who were dying: those tending the sick were contracting diseases and dying also.

In December and January those being culled from the lists of potential work scheme clients were told they should be tilling their land, a ridiculous suggestion in the depth of winter. By March, when the number of people engaged on the schemes had reached over 700,000, there was a shortage of labour available for tilling which meant that few potatoes were sown in the spring of 1847. Some landlords encouraged their tenants to sow alternative crops like carrots and turnips. Seed was supplied at cost (meaning the landlord did not profit from the sale of such seed, but the tenant still had to find whatever amount the merchant charged). It was accompanied by advice on the best way to prepare the soil and husband the crop. Some landlords even waived the rent payable by farmers who were prepared to allocate sufficient of their land to the cultivation of such crops and their proper husbandry. This was another area in which the Quakers provided a lead, offering seed and training to farmers willing to convert to alternative crops.

Nevertheless, the potatoes that were grown were healthy and by the time of the general election in August 1847 there was a feeling in many quarters that the crisis was over. The famine did not feature heavily in the campaign in Ireland, even in the most affected districts. The debate between those in favour of the Union and those advocating repeal exercised the minds of the candidates to a far greater extent than the dire conditions of their least well off constituents, few of whom were entitled to vote.

In September the soup kitchens were closed and relief confined to distribution of cash hand-outs via the PLUs. The full implications of this new system of relief were yet to reveal themselves. Whilst the new arrangements permitted the delivery of assistance to destitute individuals without insisting they become inmates of the workhouses, although they had to attend there in order to be assessed and to receive relief, a new definition of destitution included the requirement that the applicant yield all but a quarter acre of his land holding. Many landlords took advantage of this clause in the Act to embark on a series of mass evictions.

At the same time, the burden of paying for relief fell upon the same landlords who now had no income from rents with which to meet their obligations. A clear conflict of interest for those landlords who formed the bulk of the relief committee membership.

As has already been stated, people were dying in increasing numbers, from hunger, from disease and from physical decline caused by the combination of hard labour and inadequate nourishment. Even greater numbers were leaving the island in search of better conditions. Most headed either for Liverpool or Glasgow. Both cities already had significant populations of Irish who provided cheap labour for the ports and other industries associated with them. Liverpool, in particular, was a staging post en-route to North America. Around two thirds of the 250,000 who arrived in Liverpool in 1847 re-embarked for New York, Boston and New Brunswick. Some were given free passages for the 'privilege' of providing ballast on otherwise empty vessels that had brought Canadian timber to Liverpool.

Those who remained in both ports often became a burden on the parishes, the workhouses and the fever hospitals. Some were sent back to Ireland, though many of these made their way back to Liverpool some while later. The existing communities of Irish migrants were already living in squalid conditions, overcrowded, some in cellars subjected to frequent flooding.

There were frequent occurrences of typhus and cholera and the blame for these inevitably fell upon the Irish migrants. In 1847, there were 30,000 deaths from typhus across England and Wales and a further 13,000 from influenza. Dysentery was also widespread.

In Liverpool three large sheds were rented to accommodate fever patients and four vessels were requisitioned as floating hospitals to receive typhus victims of which there were around 60,000 in the city in 1847.

The English poor law, like that operating in Ireland, depended on locally raised taxes. An influx of destitute Irish placed a heavy strain on a system already struggling with high levels of poverty among the indigenous population. Inevitably sympathy for the Irish quickly waned to be replaced by resentment.

The fate of the majority of people arriving in Liverpool, those who boarded vessels bound for North America, was hardly any better. To begin with, conditions on the boats plying between English and Irish ports and North America were appalling, characterised by over-crowded and insanitary accommodation, ideal for the transmission and nurturing of all manner of infectious diseases. Around 53,000 arrived in New York in 1847 and approximately 90,000 in the St Lawrence estuary.

The authorities in New York established a quarantine station on Staten Island where people were examined. Those showing obvious signs of ill health were hospitalised. Once released they gravitated towards already established Irish communities close to the dock area. Here again the conditions in which they lived, at least to begin with, were not unlike those already described for Liverpool.

The St. Lawrence river estuary is iced up throughout the winter months. Boats heading from the British Isles to Canada therefore plied only between April and October, the first sailings taking place early in April to arrive in May. These boats would be loaded with timber for the return leg, the purpose for which they were originally intended. The adaptations made to enable the accommodation of a human cargo were minimal. Inevitably, those who survived the 4-8 week journey across the Atlantic – and a significant proportion died whilst en-route – were in a poor condition. By the end of the sailing season in 1847, nearly one fifth of those who set sail from the British Isles for North America died, either en-route, or shortly after arrival.

The Canadian quarantine station was based on an island about 40 kilometres downstream from Quebec city called Grosse Isle. The authorities there expected a significant increase in the number of boats arriving in 1847 over the number they had dealt with the previous summer and made preparations accordingly. Their estimates were woefully inadequate however.

As in New York, people who presented with obvious signs of sickness were hospitalised. And, as in New York and Liverpool, additional accommodation, usually consisting of commandeered warehouses or hastily erected sheds, was acquired for the purpose. Typhus, cholera and dysentery were the most common conditions that were endemic on the boats. Such sicknesses can have a long incubation period – up to ten days in the case of typhus for example – during which the carrier is able to pass on his or her infection. So individuals cleared by the medical authorities as healthy could still pass infection on as they continued their journey to their final destination.

From Quebec City, immigrants travelled first to Montreal where, once again, the sick were accommodated in temporary hospitals. The comparatively healthy then travelled onwards, south into the USA or further north or west. The journey west took them first to Kingston, where Lake Ontario discharges into the St Lawrence, and thence to Toronto from where they would continue their journey over land.

At the time, a settlement of barely 20,000 souls, Toronto found itself having to cope with an influx of 38,500 immigrants, three quarters of whom were Irish, during the summer of 1847. The journey time, along the length of Lake Ontario, lasted several days by barge. At some point the authorities commandeered faster vessels that reduced the journey time to around 5 days.

In the United States and Canada, it fell to the local communities to raise the necessary funding in order to cope with the growing crisis. In Canada this certainly led to some degree of resentment, less so in New York and Boston where there were already significant numbers of Irish immigrants with both the will and the means to assist their fellow countrymen. Indeed, many were already collecting subscriptions which they remitted to Ireland to assist with the relief effort there.

Chapter 11 – Autumn-Winter 1847/8

In late summer of 1847 it might have seemed to some, as it had one year previously, that the crisis was, if not over, certainly coming to an end. How else is it possible to explain the lack of attention paid to the famine during the election that August? Certainly the potato crop appeared to be healthy. What does not seem to have been appreciated until much too late is that the quantity of potatoes planted the previous spring was significantly smaller than in previous years, far too little to meet the needs of a hungry population, even one depleted by disease and emigration.

Whilst the candidates standing for election in Ireland had little to say about the most visible problem faced by their constituents, the authorities in London certainly took precautions designed to limit the effect of any possible hostility the candidates might encounter. To help understand this it is worth digressing briefly to explain the practice of law enforcement that had developed over preceding decades both in Ireland and in mainland Britain. We have already seen that Robert Peel was the British Prime Minister at the time of the outbreak of famine in Ireland. He is best remembered in England for the creation of the Metropolitan Police whilst he was Home Secretary 15 years before. His name is immortalised in the nicknames given to the force – *Peelers* and, later, *Bobbies*.

Law enforcement had previously been in the hands of local

constables appointed by magistrates and supported, when deemed necessary, by military force. A similar situation pertained in Ireland, with a force known as Watchmen covering Dublin, and Baronial Constabulary operating in each county. Under an agreement between Peel and Henry Goulborn, the Irish Secretary, a new Irish Constabulary was established in 1822.

The army, however, continued to play an important role in law enforcement in Ireland. Landlords were happy to sell land to the Government for the establishment of barracks and welcomed the extra security that the presence of soldiers provided. There were a total of 15,000 soldiers stationed in Ireland in 1843. That figure almost doubled to 29,500 by 1849, around 82% of all troops stationed in the British Isles at the time. A significant part of that increase was introduced in the summer of 1847 to provide security for the election candidates.

More generally they assisted landlords in enforcing the payment of rents, the protection of convoys of grain being transported to the ports, and the eviction of tenants. No town of any significance was without its military barracks.

The new arrangements, consisting of the closure of soup kitchens to be replaced by direct provision of cash hand-outs to the most destitute, enabling them to purchase food, were incapable of coping with the extent of the demands placed upon them. Late in 1847 The Poor Law Commission declared 20 PLUs to be "distressed" in recognition that the resources available to them were inadequate to meet the demand expected to be encountered. Poor Law Inspectors were appointed. These individuals were required to work with the Boards of Guardians to ensure that the rates – the levy imposed on land holders to fund the work of the PLUs – were collected. They also, like the Public Works Inspectors before them, were charged with ensuring that assistance was provided only to those who qualified under the new, more stringent, conditions and that there was no favouritism. Often this brought them into direct conflict with the Guardians.

The PLU administered from Kilrush in County Clare was one of those Unions designated as distressed. The man appointed as inspector was a former army captain, who had already seen service in the army in Ireland in the run up to the election. The fourth son of a protestant landowner from Cultra on the shores of Belfast Lough, Arthur Kennedy would have had much in common with Crofton Vandeleur the proprietor of Kilrush and chairman of the Board of Guardians. Nevertheless, the relationship between the two men quickly became soured and in March the Board was disbanded with the Inspector taking charge.

It was now, as winter approached, that serious unrest began to break out. One morning in December a crowd of up to 1000 turned up outside the gates to the Kilrush workhouse. Many had marched from the outlying villages to demand that the distribution of assistance commence. The new regime for the first time authorised the distribution of relief to able-bodied individuals without the requirement they be admitted to the workhouse, although they had to come to the workhouse to receive it. At Kilrush this had not yet begun, the Guardians insisting that people be admitted to the workhouse in order to receive relief, a policy with which Captain Kennedy concurred, there not being sufficient money available because all of the rates due had yet to be collected. The army was called and successfully dispersed most of the throng.

On the last day of December a crudely written note was posted on the gate to Vandeleur's residence threatening the lives of both men. These events, and others like them elsewhere, were attributed to a group called "Young Irelanders". This organisation was an offshoot of O'Connell's Repeal Association whose formal name was The Irish Confederation. Consisting of both Catholic and Protestant intellectuals and politicians, it advocated greater Catholic emancipation and a widening of the franchise.

1848 was a year of turmoil across Europe, with revolutions taking place in France, Germany, Austria, Denmark and the Netherlands. In February the last vestige of the French Royal family fled France never to return. Inspired by this, a Young Ireland delegation led by William Smith O'Brien and Thomas Francis Meagher, went in April to Paris to meet with representatives of the new French Republic. Whilst there they were given a flag modelled on the French *Tricoleur* on which the three colours that were represented were green, the colour of Catholic nationalism, orange, the colour of Protestant unionism, separated by white to signify the desire for peace between the two traditions. Since 1922 this has been the national flag of the Irish Republic.

For leaders of the Confederation, the fact that the 1848 French revolution had been relatively bloodless was an inspiration and they hoped to be able to mobilise people from all strata of Irish society in a bid to return government of the Irish to Ireland. One of the ways they set out to achieve this was via a newspaper called *The Nation*. However, the authorities quickly took action to nip the Confederation's activities in the bud. We shall return to this subject later, since it was in the summer of 1848 that things came to a head and this chapter is meant to be dealing only with the preceding winter.

As the winter progressed more and more people faced destitution. This was the third winter of fatally depleted resources. People who had struggled through more than two years of unbelievable hardship, selling every possession in order to provide the barest necessities of life, had nothing left. From labouring on the work schemes of 1846/7, from standing in line to receive often watery soup; after pawning their winter clothing, selling, or eating, their last pig or skeletal cow; they now faced another winter of grubbing in the mud for turnips or begging for the few coins dispensed by a near bankrupt Union. In order to qualify it was necessary for them to give up their last vestige of dignity – the family home. Often as not the choice was forced upon them, for landlords like Vandeleur now began evicting tenants, and not only those who were in arrears of rent.

In the spring of 1848, the Quakers, who had distributed 35,196 lbs of seeds in May of 1847, now distributed close to 130,000 lbs in over 143,000 individual grants across twenty-four counties. The only requirement was that the recipient had land ready. They even rented 572 acres of land in County Mayo for diverse food crops and flax to establish the linen industry in the west.

In government, determination to blame landowners and to insist that they should meet the costs of alleviating the suffering of their fellow countrymen was once again asserted. The Secretary to the Treasury, Charles Trevelyan, suggested that landlords should improve their estates under the Land Improvement Act and at the same time pay the increasing burden of rates, "or dispose of their estates to those who can perform this indispensable duty"[1]

Chapter 12 – Summer 1848 and After

One of Daniel O'Connell's protégés, Cork land-owner and lawyer Feargus O'Connor, was elected MP for Cork in 1832. Shortly afterwards he fell out with O'Connell and in 1835 lost his seat in Parliament. He then embarked on a campaign for political reform in England. Founding a newspaper, *The Northern Star,* he was joined by William Lovett and others. Their People's Charter was published - in May 1838 - as a draft parliamentary bill. It contained six points: manhood suffrage; the ballot; abolition of property qualifications for MPs; payment of MPs; equal electoral districts; and annual elections. Thousands of working people had rallied together on the basis of this charter, and hundreds of them had gone to prison for their beliefs.

In the 1847 general election O'Connor was elected MP for Nottingham. By the spring of 1848, inspired by events elsewhere in Europe, the movement was ready to make its mark. A petition had been raised, signed, it was claimed, by over 5 million people. A meeting was arranged for April 10th on Kennington Common just across the Thames from Parliament.

The government was well prepared with 170,000 citizens signed up as special constabulary and army units stationed at the entrance to each of the bridges and protecting ministries and ministers' homes. Despite an expected turn-out of 200,000, a mere 20,000 congregated. When it began to rain heavily, most quickly disbursed. O'Connor and his henchmen crossed Westminster Bridge in horse drawn carriages and presented his petition which was found to contain only 2 million names, many of them forged, invented and duplicated. The name of no less a figure than the Duke of Wellington appeared 17 times.

This attempted English revolution descended into farce, but the authorities were alerted to the possibility of something similar occurring in Ireland. Three of the leaders of the Irish Confederation were arrested and charged with treason. In May, having been found guilty, they were sentenced to 14 years transportation. Before this punishment could be put into effect, its imposition provided the impetus for a recruitment campaign leading to a potential rebellion.

On 29th July O'Brien led the siege of a cottage in Ballingarry, County Tipperary, in which some members of the constabulary had taken refuge. One of his men was killed by a random shot fired from within the cottage and O'Brien led his men away. He was arrested shortly afterwards at Thurles railway station.

One of the men who had accompanied O'Brien to Paris in April, Richard O'Gorman, was organiser for the rebellion in Limerick. A few days after the Ballngarry incident, a group of about 200 men, supposedly acting on behalf of O'Gorman, held up the Limerick-Tralee mail coach at Abbeyfeale. They confiscated the arms and official dispatches it contained but returned private mail to the postmaster. They considered mounting a siege of the town but, when they heard the news from Tipperary decided to call a halt.

O'Gorman disappeared. Two different speculative accounts of his escape from arrest, include the possibility that he travelled via Kilrush. Indeed, two men were arrested and accused of transporting him aboard a steamer bound for the town. A less likely tale has him aboard another Kilrush bound steamer disguised as a woman.

Whatever the fate of O'Gorman and the other conspirators, there can be no doubt that the rebellion, if not quite as farcical as that in England, nevertheless fizzled out for lack of support. It did nothing to help relieve the suffering of those who had neither food nor the means to acquire it except by sacrificing what few possessions they had. On the contrary, it served to harden public opinion in England where the Irish were already being viewed as ungrateful.

That country was already experiencing an economic crisis caused by a variety of factors other than the Irish famine. A bubble in railway construction share prices had burst. Late in 1847, in an attempt to increase the availability of credit, the Bank of England had suspended rules that meant loans could not be provided unless backed by gold. Shortages of raw cotton from the southern states of the USA, combined with a lack of credit, caused several textile mills to close with a consequent increase in unemployment. Irish migrants arriving in industrial centres thus afflicted were not welcome.

Pressure to introduce an Encumbered Estates measure now increased. Having been introduced in the spring of 1847 and withdrawn under pressure from insurance companies and other mortgagors it was reintroduced in February 1848, the Lord Chancellor stating his belief that "it was impossible for a landlord, whose income arising from his landed estate was intercepted by mortgages and other charges, to perform those duties which a landlord should perform"[1]. The bill was intended to remove, or at the very least reduce the extent of the holdings of, the existing proprietors of Irish land, replacing them with people willing to invest in the improvement of the land. Such improvement, of course, would necessitate the removal of the many occupiers of small holdings, and cottiers.

Further amendments to the Poor Law Extension Act were enacted. These included authorising PLUs to provide grants to the destitute to enable them emigrate, a measure under which solvent PLUs were expected to bail out insolvent ones, and the construction of 33 more workhouses.

Assisted emigration had long been a practice of many landlords, especially in relation to colonisation of the antipodes. The particular scheme under which Pat Lillis's ancestor, Mary Marrinan, left for Australia was instituted by Earl Grey in 1848. At the time he was Secretary of State for the Colonies, in which role he would have been well aware of the imbalance between the sexes in Australia. Between October 1848 and August 1850, more than 4,000 Irish girls, aged mainly between fourteen and nineteen years, sailed on eleven Australia-bound ships[2]. The girls, all supposedly orphans, were workhouse inmates.

On the voyages they were under the supervision of a surgeon superintendent. Each was fitted out with a 'uniform' consisting of two gowns, six shifts, six pairs of stockings, two pairs of shoes and various other items. One can only assume that the majority of these clothes were stored on the voyage for, although conditions on board were certainly much more salubrious than those endured by most migrants, it seems improbable that the wearing of gowns would have been appropriate at any time during 122 days at sea in all weathers.

Many of these girls became the wives of farmers to whom they bore large numbers of children. One is an ancestor of the former Australian Prime Minister, Kevin Rudd. Mary Marrinan, however, returned to Ireland some six years after her arrival there.

The blight returned in the autumn of 1848, once again destroying most of the crop. An epidemic of cholera caused many deaths right across the United Kingdom in the winter of 1848/9. In Ireland, people, weakened by lack of food and exposure to the elements following eviction, readily succumbed to such diseases, including dysentery. The prevalence of an assortment of diseases in many workhouses made people reluctant to enter them. Even so, overcrowding within them continued.

Blight struck yet again in 1849, though not with the same

intensity. Distress and destitution continued, along with evictions and migration, for a number of years.

In July and August of 1849 the historian, essayist and social critic Thomas Carlyle toured Ireland. Having seen the condition of Irish immigrants in Glasgow and Liverpool he wanted to see for himself the realities of what they were leaving behind. He chose as his travelling companion one of the leaders of the Young Ireland movement, Charles Gavan Duffy. Carlyle was opposed to Duffy's movement and to the repeal movement in general. Nevertheless, Duffy and his colleagues were impressed by Carlyle's support for social reform.

Although his writings about what he saw were not published until after his death they tell us how horrified he was by what he saw. His descriptions of the cities, towns and villages through which he passed on a journey that took him from Dublin, through Kildare, Carlow and Kilkenny to Waterford and, thence, along the coast to Cork, west to Kilarney then north to Limerick, Galway, Westport, Sligo, Letterkenny and Derry, are full of despair at the extent of the poverty he witnessed. He condemned landlords, the Liberal government and the Poor Law, holding them collectively responsible for the parlous state of affairs.

Like many of his contemporaries he saw the potato blight as an opportunity to end the population's dependence on that particular crop, arguing for improvement through the provision of work. He reserved his strongest criticism for the workhouses, calling them a vile imposition which had turned society into a breeding ground for pauperism.

In 1851, whilst part of the United Kingdom was being ravaged by hunger and disease, the government mounted a showcase of its achievements. The Great Exhibition was staged in a gigantic glass house, dubbed The Crystal Palace, and attracted tens of thousands of visitors from across the Empire.

It would be possible to pepper this book with scores of accounts featuring terrible human tragedies. They can be found in countless contemporaneous documents, from that of Asenath Nicholson, already referred to, to many reports from visiting journalists in such organs as *The Illustrated London News*, and to numerous reports submitted to the Poor Law Commissioners by inspectors like Arthur Kennedy, and the reports of several Parliamentary inquiries that took place. The problem is that there are so many that choosing to highlight a few would be to imply that others, some perhaps yet untold, were less tragic.

That a million people died, out of a population of between 8 and 9 million in a period of just 5 years, in addition to the underlying 'normal' death rate; that they often died in terrible conditions; that at the height of the famine in 1847 and '48 many were buried in multi-occupancy graves with the minimum of ceremony; that many more survived, having experienced intense hunger and disease under the jurisdiction of a nation justifiably proud of its achievements, at the apex of its success, should be a source of shame to every citizen of that nation. Those who, 170 years on, proclaim their pride in those achievements need to be reminded that, at a time when it was leading the campaign against slavery in the USA, Britain's government oversaw a tragedy of historic proportions on soil it claimed as its own.

Part 3 – Conclusions

Chapter 13 – Summing Up

The use of first person singular in this chapter acknowledges that what follows are the personal views of Frank Parker, not necessarily shared by his co-author, Patrick Lillis.

I remember discussions with Irish acquaintances shortly after my arrival in Ireland in which I had the effrontery to respond to criticisms of the way the Irish were treated by the British in the past. My view, back then, was that it was wrong to lay the blame collectively at the British. Rather, it was the ruling classes, the aristocracy, who were to blame, and that those same people, or their fellows, treated ordinary British citizens just as badly. They had children working in the mines and mills; the lower classes worked long hours for little reward, living in awful conditions in slums in the industrial cities, or in tied farm cottages with inadequate facilities in rural areas.

Reading about the famine I am forced to revise my opinion. I think differently now, too, about the stone walls that surround so many Irish properties. I cringe when I recall the crass remark I made to my Northern Irish brother-in-law about the Irish 'loving their stone walls'. He did not retort, as he might have done, that many were built by destitute men whose families would have starved to death had they not been provided with such labour. On my Sunday morning cycle rides, when I come across a wall that seems to go on for miles, I wonder about its builders and the conditions under which they worked. Did they provide their labour in lieu of rent? Did the landowner provide the work in what he would have deemed to be an act of generosity, ensuring the recipient enjoyed the dignity of work when the alternative was the degradation that accompanies the act of begging for food? Did the landowner pressurise the administrators of the public works scheme to carry out the work on his property?

I now know that the conditions the Irish had to endure were far worse than those experienced by the majority of ordinary English, Scots or Welsh men, women and children. This book has been an attempt to understand why, and to convey that understanding to as many as are minded to read it. It's sub-title, implying, as it is intended to do, that Liberalism played a crucial part in the tragedy, is part of the answer. And it is one that it is painful for me, a life long Liberal, to admit.

The words 'colonisation' and 'violence' frequently occur in Irish accounts of the period. The first is used pejoratively by people who see the process of occupation and attempted assimilation of the native Irish by the English as inherently evil. I hope I have succeeded in demonstrating that that process, whilst setting the context for the disaster, was not a cause of it. It was, after all, a process that had been on-going for 8 centuries before the arrival of potato blight. Many of the descendants of invading occupiers regarded themselves as Irish and still do. We have seen how, following the repeal of the penal laws and the restoration to

Irish Catholics of the right to practice their religion, it was sometimes Protestant landowners who provided the land and the funds to enable the building of Catholic churches in many communities, including in Belfast.

The reality of the Williamite success in the Battle of the Boyne, far from being, as some of Northern Ireland's Protestant community would have us believe, a victory of Protestant over Catholic, was celebrated in the Vatican with a thanksgiving mass, demonstrating that the motives of its leaders had far more to do with pan-European politics than with religion.

We can see that organisations like Young Ireland were led by Protestant as well as Catholic men. The Irish Tricoleur is meant to represent the two religious traditions linked by a desire for peace between them. So it is wrong to suggest – as many English politicians and officials did at the time and Irish Republicans do today – that the Irish are a different race from the English.

The truth is that, Britain's planned exit from the EU notwithstanding, we are all Europeans.

And the truth of the Great Irish Famine is that it was mostly to do with attitudes to poverty.

But, whilst 'colonisation' is, in my view, an inappropriate word to use in connection with the causes of Ireland's suffering, 'violence' certainly is not. In fact, I would argue that the famine represents one of the most violent and painful manifestations of the transition from a subsistence economy to a cash economy, a transition which had already taken place across much of the rest of Europe.

The cottiers and small-holders who worked for farmers and their landlords, on those occasions when labour was needed, in return for the right to occupy a small plot on which to grow potatoes, needed little cash beyond what was required to purchase seeds and the materials to make some rough clothing. A modern trading economy requires people to earn a regular income with which to purchase the products of industry. The transition from one to the other, however achieved, is bound to leave some individuals behind, prominent among them the weak and the poorly educated.

Another word that occurs frequently in accounts of the famine is 'improvement'. Whilst not used pejoratively, there often seems to be in some Irish versions, an underlying suggestion that improvement, in the context of agrarian reform, is not necessarily a good thing. The concept of improvement lies at the heart of Liberalism. To achieve the greatest good for the greatest number is its ultimate objective. The realisation of this objective, in the eighteenth and nineteenth centuries, was perceived to lie in the peaceful transformation of lives and livelihoods through the application of scientific discoveries, accompanied by social reorganisation. Incomes could be increased by increasing productivity through mechanisation of manufacturing processes on the one hand, and drainage and cultivation of the land on the other. Hand in hand with this went the belief that education, equipping people with knowledge and skills, was the key to lifting people from subsistence into greater affluence.

But we have seen how mechanisation of textile production deprived home based spinners and weavers of their livelihoods and how the introduction of more profitable crops and livestock necessitated the removal of small holders and cottiers from the land. This was, of course, accompanied with the belief that encouraging such individuals to leave Ireland for new lives in North America or the Antipodes would provide them with the opportunity of a better life in those new lands.

The belief that the proprietors of Irish land were the true villains, taking rents, using the land as security for loans, used not for investment but to indulge in all manner of selfish pursuits, from gambling to the 'buying' of political favours, was, and remains, widespread on all sides. But, whilst many landowners did indeed bleed their estates dry, there were others who not only provided work and accommodation for tenants in the years leading up to the famine, but continued to do so throughout the famine.

To Liberals, however, from those like the Young Irelanders who sought the repeal of the Act of Union in order to secure a fairer distribution of land, to the Quakers who espoused a form of Christianity in which every man had the right to an equal share of the product of his labour, it was axiomatic that any landlord who had become so indebted that he was unable to shoulder his share of the burden of relieving the suffering of his tenants ought to have that land taken from him. In the words of Charles Trevelyan, quoted in chapter 11: landlords should improve their estates under the Land Improvement Act and at the same time pay the increasing burden of rates, "or dispose of their estates to those who can perform this indispensable duty".

Introducing such measures, however well intended, would bring about suffering for some at the best of times, as they did elsewhere in Europe, often becoming the spark for revolution. To impose them in the midst of a famine of unprecedented proportions was a recipe for disaster. And that disaster was further exacerbated by the imposition of conditions for the receipt of relief that sought to distinguish between the 'deserving' and 'undeserving' poor.

It is a distinction that we continue to make 170 years later in our attempts to address poverty. We no longer force people to endure the hardships of the workhouse, but we do expect people to actively seek employment in order to receive benefits. And we have, throughout the developed world, a sizeable bureaucracy dedicated to weeding out those claimants in receipt of benefits to which the rules of the system dictate that they are not entitled.

The statement in Chapter 7, that anyone in receipt of the fruits of another's labour has a duty to expend an equivalent amount of his own labour in return, is a truism. But, if the economic system is unable to provide opportunities for that exchange to take place, that system is broken and needs to be mended. The custodians of the system in nineteenth century Britain recognised, not that the system was broken, perhaps, but that it was not yet fully developed. Their remedy, the taxing of supposedly wealthy individuals the majority of whom lacked the capacity to pay, failed to achieve the desired end.

Another word that appears frequently in Irish Republican discourse about the famine is 'genocide'. The United Nations defines genocide as *"acts committed with intent to destroy, in whole or in part, a national, ethnical, racial or religious group."* To fit this definition to the disaster inflicted on Ireland in the mid 1800s requires two things: intent, and an acceptance that those who suffered were different, as a group, from the rest of the inhabitants of the British Isles. It is certainly incontestible that the government's intention was to evince a reduction in the population of Ireland. Its destruction, even in part, was not, I believe, intended. Destruction in part was undoubtedly a by-product of misguided policies but it was not their aim.

That the portion of the population that endured the greatest losses was of a particular religious group is undeniable, as is the fact that certain Protestant preachers sought to convert as many as possible to what they regarded as the 'true faith', sometimes making it a condition for the receipt of relief. But many Protestants suffered also. Followers of the 'old' religion were not deliberately singled out for destruction. So the accusation that the famine was a deliberate act of genocide cannot be sustained by the available evidence.

It is unreasonable to condemn the Russell government's response to the famine without offering suggestions as to alternative courses of action. The suspension of brewing and exports of grain and other food products, proposed by O'Connell and others, was rejected at the time because the government was averse to anything that would interfere with the natural working of markets. It is worth pointing out, too, that not only would it have produced food shortages in mainland Britain, it would have put many Irish people out of work, depriving them of the ability to purchase any additional food that became available as a result.

One of the lessons learned since the second world war, if not before, is the importance of extensive state support for agriculture. The most successful of the measures introduced in Ireland during the famine were those by the Quakers, and certain enlightened landlords, that encouraged and enabled farmers to grow alternative crops. The second thing that has been practiced effectively in recent decades is the one advocated three Millenia ago in the Old Testament: the storage of surpluses from good years to ensure a continuing supply in times of poor yields. One of the perceived benefits of a union of nations, whether the supposedly United Kingdom of Britain and Ireland in the nineteenth century, or more recent organisations like the European Union, is the ability to tax the more successful regions of the union in order to support the economic development of the less successful. That did not happen in the UK at the time. Instead the burden of relieving Irish poverty fell almost exclusively on the owners of Irish land.

The extent to which such a combination of measures might have helped the situation, if adopted by Russell's government, can only be speculated about. The taxing of Irish landowners and confiscation of those estates with unsustainable debt burdens did achieve long term benefits for many of the famine's survivors. Certainly in the short term there was great suffering. But in the years following the famine the break up of large estates and the expansion of medium sized holdings by the acquisition of small holdings abandoned by emigrants did contribute to an increase in the prosperity of many Irish families. And many of those migrants did find better lives in their new homelands. But the existence of poverty alongside affluence continued everywhere and is as prevalent today.

The fundamental problem identified by Malthus has not been solved. Certainly he never envisioned the possibility of the world's population reaching 7.5 billion[1], nor would he have been able to imagine that it would be possible to grow sufficient food to feed such a number. Not only are we now able to produce enough food, we waste vast quantities. But, in doing so, and in transporting it across the oceans, we are slowly destroying the planet. We can grow food in tunnels beneath the ground; we can 'farm' insects; both are being done in Britain today. But unrestrained population growth must inevitably outpace food production. The planet is finite. Malthus's predictions may not have come true yet, but one day they must.

That day may be closer than we think. Famine still stalks parts of Africa. It still follows wars that continue to rage with the same intensity as in the past. Whereas, in the past, wars were the result of disputes between members of the aristocracy over the right to occupy land, often disguised behind claims that one religion was superior to another, today the aristocracy has been replaced by great corporations, the acquisition of land by control of resources. And, still, religion is often the false pretext.

Unless and until we can find a way both to conserve resources and to distribute them more uniformly among the people, unless we can end the relentless increase in population which continues despite the depredation of wars and famines, we can never achieve that dream of the "greatest good for the greatest number" beloved of Liberals the world over. I am reminded again of Charles Woods's words which gave this book its title and which looked forward to the possibility of "quiet and prosperity" following a period of "misery and starvation". For all too brief a period after the second World War it might have seemed that ideal had been achieved, at least for the majority of those of us fortunate to live in the developed world. Looking at the state of the world today, it is evident that many are still experiencing a purgatory of misery. It is the duty of progressive politicians everywhere to develop and implement compassionate policies towards such people wherever they are.

References

Chapter 1

1. English pipe rolls, quoted by James Lydon in *The Lordsip of Ireland in the Middle Ages,* Gill and McMillan, Mar.1972.

2. Annals of Connaught quoted by Adrian Martyn in *One King to Rule them All – Edward Bruce and the Battle of Athenry 1316* at The Irish Story (on-line publication)

3. *A View of the present State of Ireland*, Edmund Spencer, 1596

Chapter 2

1. Fea , Alan: *Secret Chambers and Hidiing Places*, Dodo Press, 2008 (first published 1901)

2. York, Philip Chasney (1911). *"Strafford, Thomas Wentworth, Earl of"*. In Chisholm, Hugh. *Encyclopædia Britannica. 25 (11th ed.).* Cambridge University Press. pp. 978–980

3. The words of Oliver Cromwell, quoted by Simon Schama in *The British Wars 1603-1776, Vol.2 of A History of Britain* BBC Worldwide Ltd., 2001

4. Connolly, James: *Labour in Irish History* (1910)

Chapter 3

1. *Factsheet on the Irish Agricultural and Food & Drink Sector*, Bord Bia, 2017

Chapter 4

1.   Keenan, Desmond: *Ireland 1800-1850*, Xlibris, 2002.

2.   Delaney, P.J.: *The tragic sinking of the Francis Spaight,* Writing.com, 2015 (Original source not provided)

3.   Various newspapers reported the incident during 1836, including accounts from various crew members of the Angenora.

Chapter 6

1.   *The Wealth of Nations*, Adam Smith (1776)

2.   *An Essay on the Principle of Population*, Thomas Malthus (1798)

Chapter 7

1.   Kelly, James: *Scarcity and Poor Relief in Eighteenth-Century Ireland: The Subsistence Crisis of 1782-4,* Irish Historical Studies, Vol. 28, No. 109 (May, 1992)

2.   Nicholls, George: *Poor Laws – Ireland: Three Reports by George Nicholls Esq. To Her Majesty's Principal Secretary of State for Home Department* (London, 1838)

Chapter 8

1.   Nyaradi, Annett; Li, Jianhong; Hickling, Siobhan; Foster, Jonathan; and Oddy, Wendy H: *The role of nutrition in children's neurocognitive development, from pregnancy through childhood* in *Frontiers in Neuroscience*, March 2013.

Chapter 9

1. Nicholson, Asenath: *Lights and Shade of Ireland*, (London, 1850)

2. Graham to Peel, September 6, 1843, in C. S.Parker, *Sir Robert Peel from his Private Papers*, iii, p.63. Quoted in Lane, Padraig G, *The Encumbered Estates Court, Ireland, 1848-1849*, Paper published at tcd.ie, being derived from Lane's MA thesis of 1969.

Chapter 10

1. See O'Murchada, Ciaran: *Figures in a Famine Landscape*, Bloomsbury Academic, 2016, chapter 2

2. *ibid*

3. Captain Coffin of H.M.S *Scourge* in a letter to Charles Trevelyan in February 1847, quoted in *Atlas Of The Great Irish Famine*, Cork University Press, 2012

4. Unnamed sailor from H.M.S *Tartarus, ibid*

5. Quoted by Wesley Johnston in *The Ireland Story* at wesleyjohntson.com

Chapter 11

1. Trevelyan to Twistelton, December 14, 1847, PLB. Vol. XVIII, as quoted in C. Woodham-Smith, *The Great Hunger* and cited by Lane, Padraig G, *The Encumbered Estates Court, Ireland, 1848-1849, op.cit.*

Chapter 12

1. Lord Clarendon's speech introducing the Encumbered Estates Bill, 1848, to parliament, quoted in Lane, Padraig G, *The Encumbered Estates Court, Ireland, 1848-1849,*

op.cit.

2. Keneally, Thomas, *The Great Famine and Australia* in *Atlas Of The Great Irish Famine*, Cork University Press, 2012

Chapter 13

1. Correct as at 23rd September 2017. For an up to date figure see

http://www.worldometers.info/world-population/

Bibliography

In addition to the sources referenced above, of which *The Atlas of The Great Irish Famine* is the most comprehensive single reference source, the following books offer further facts and opinions about the event and its context.

The Great Hunger: Ireland: 1845- 1849; Cecil Woodham-Smith, Pub. Hamish Hamilton (UK), Harper (USA), 1962

The Great Irish Potato Famine; James S Donnelly, Jr., Pub. History Press, 2002

The Famine Plot: England's Role in Ireland's Greatest Tragedy: Tim Pat Coogan, Pub. St. Martin's Press, 2012

Black Potatoes: The Story of The Great Irish Famine, 1845- 1850: Susan Campbell Bartoletti, Pub. Houghton Mifflin Harcourt, 2001 (The only book on the subject specifically targeted at young readers)

The Graves are Walking: The Great Famine and the Saga of the Irish People: John Kelly, Pub. Henry Holt and Company, 2012

The Great Irish Famine: A History in Four Lives; Enda Delaney, Pub. Gill, 2014

Famine Echoes, Cathal Poirteir, Pub. Gill & Macmillan, 1995

The Great Shame: Thomas Kenneally, Pub. Knopf Doubleday, 2010

Famine, Land and Politics: British Government and Irish Society, 1843-1850: Peter Grey, Pub. Irish Academic Press, 1999.

Receiving Erin's Children: Philadelphia, Liverpool and the Irish Famine Migration, 1845-1855, James Matthew Gallman, Pub. Univ. Of North Carolina Press, 2000

The Great Famine: Ireland's Agony 1845-1852: Ciaran O Murchadha, Pub. A & C Black, 2011

The End of Hidden Ireland: Rebellion, Famine, and Emigration: Robert James Scally, Pub. Oxford University Press, 1995

This Great Calamity; The Irish Famine 1845-1852: Christine Kinealy, Pub. Roberts Rinehart, 1997

Black '47 and Beyond: The Great Irish Famine in History, Economy and Memory: Cormac O Grada, Pub. Princeton University Press, 2000.

Great Famine: Ireland's Potato Famine, 1845-51: John Percival, Diane Pub. Co., 1995.

About the Authors

Frank Parker is a retired Engineer fascinated by the history of his adopted land - Ireland. He is the author of four novels. His short stories have appeared in several anthologies. He blogs at https://franklparker.com

Patrick Lillis holds a degree in Agricultural Science and worked as an agricultural advisor for the Irish government and for an agricultural finance organisation. He also ran his own real estate agency before becoming interested in genealogy and family history.

Both reside in County Laois.

Made in the USA
Columbia, SC
15 May 2018